Soul Mates
- & -
Hot Dates

D1112924

Maria Shaw is a celebrity astrologer and the author of eight books. She has appeared on *VH1, Fox News, E! Entertainment, Life & Style,* the *Oxygen Channel, Blind Date,* and many other national programs. Maria is also the love and sex columnist for *Complete Woman* magazine and is the astrologer for *Soap Opera Digest, TigerBeat,* and *Bop!* Her weekly radio show, *Affairs of the Heart,* draws thousands of listeners, and her current lecture tour takes her across the country to New York, Los Angeles, Minneapolis, Ft. Lauderdale, New Orleans, and San Francisco. Maria divides her time between two homes, in Michigan and in New Orleans' historic French Quarter.

Soul Mates
-&-
Hot Dates

How To Tell Who's Who

MAria Shaw

Llewellyn Publications
St. Paul, Minnesota

Soul Mates & Hot Dates: How to Tell Who's Who © 2005 by Maria Shaw. All rights reserved. No part of this book may be used or reproduced in any manner whatsoever, including Internet usage, without written permission from Llewellyn Publications except in the case of brief quotations embodied in critical articles and reviews.

First Edition
First Printing, 2005

Book design and format by Donna Burch
Cover design by Gavin Dayton Duffy
Edited by Andrea Neff
Llewellyn is a registered trademark of Llewellyn Worldwide, Ltd.

Library of Congress Cataloging-in-Publication Data

Shaw, Maria, 1963-.
    Soul mates & hot dates : how to tell who's who / by Maria Shaw.
        p.   cm.
    ISBN 0-7387-0746-5
    1. Astrology. 2. Soul mates. I. Title: Soul mates and hot dates. II. Title.

    BF1729.L6S42 2005
    133.5'864677—dc22   2005044101

Llewellyn Worldwide does not participate in, endorse, or have any authority or responsibility concerning private business transactions between our authors and the public.
    All mail addressed to the author is forwarded but the publisher cannot, unless specifically instructed by the author, give out an address or phone number.
    Any Internet references contained in this work are current at publication time, but the publisher cannot guarantee that a specific location will continue to be maintained. Please refer to the publisher's website for links to authors' websites and other sources.

Llewellyn Publications
A Division of Llewellyn Worldwide, Ltd.
P.O. Box 64383, Dept. 0-7387-0746-5
St. Paul, MN 55164-0383, U.S.A.
www.llewellyn.com

Printed in the United States of America

Other Books by Maria Shaw

Heart and Soul: A Karmic Love and Compatibility Guide
Mid Summer's Eve Publishing

The Enchanted Soul
Mid Summer's Eve Publishing

Welcome to Our Breakfast Table
The Olde Victorian Inn

Maria Shaw's Star Gazer
Llewellyn Publications, 2003

Maria Shaw's Tarot Kit for Teens
Llewellyn Publications, 2004

Maria Shaw's Book of Love
Llewellyn Publications, 2005

Forthcoming Books by Maria Shaw

Maria Shaw's Sun Sign Book
Llewellyn Publications

*For all of those who have found their soul mates
and those still searching*

Contents

Acknowledgments

Special thanks to my family for their support. Thanks also to my Hollywood publicist, Steve Allen, the publicity team at Llewellyn who have helped me over the years, Jill, Heather, and Allison, and also to my editor, Andrea Neff. And I can't forget all of my dear "soul friends," those special people who have touched my life in such a magnificent way over the years.

Introduction

I seem to be on this magical journey . . . a journey that has taken me around the country, meeting people of different ages and varied backgrounds. But they all have one thing in common—they believe in the theory of soul mates and past lives. I have been touring the United States holding lectures and seminars titled "Past Lives and Present Loves." I meet people with heart-touching stories about their soul mates. We have all heard the word soul mate, but what does it really mean? Through this book, I hope you will gain a deeper understanding of what we all are searching for. You may have already met your soul mate, and this book will help you confirm and appreciate the special connection you share. For those of you still searching, it is my hope that you, too, will find yourself on a magical journey that leads to true love.

—Maria

Soul Mates

Have you ever met someone and instantly fallen head over heels in love? Some of you may not believe in love at first sight, but for those of you who have experienced it, you definitely know what it feels like. Your eyes meet for the first time, your heart skips a beat, and you feel flushed, anxious, and infatuated all at the same time.

As a professional astrologer who specializes in relationships and romance, clients often ask me, "When will I meet my soul mate?"

A common misconception is that soul mates are always romantic partners. They do not necessarily have to be lovers, husbands or wives, boyfriends or girlfriends. My definition of a soul-mate connection is two souls walking the same spiritual path, working together to achieve a higher purpose or learn an important lesson.

If the person you consider to be a soul mate happens to be your lover or spouse, all the better. That makes the relationship even more special. But remember, a soul mate can be your best friend, your child, and, for you pet lovers, even man's best friend!

If you believe in the theory of reincarnation, look at soul mates this way: before you were born into this current lifetime, your soul made a contract with someone else to "hook up," to meet again or get back together.

There are several reasons souls would make such an agreement.

1. To repay a debt.

2. To receive payment of a debt.

3. To learn a lesson.

4. To right a wrong.

5. Because of an early death in a former lifetime.

6. For the soul's growth.

7. To complete or finish something.

8. To help another soul.

9. Out of love.

As I mentioned earlier, there are many different types of soul-mate connections. Here are a few of the most common.

1. Family

2. Soul groups

3. Past-life connections

4. Soul friends

5. Soul mates/lovers

The Family Connection

Most of our past-life connections are with family members. Whether you realize it or not, we choose our parents before we are born. This selection is made to assist us with working on some of the most intense issues regarding emotional security, trust, guilt, and even fear. Parents represent our very first relationships, and they give us the chance to work out our soul's lessons early in life. If we don't, we later draw lovers or partners to help us learn and complete the process. Our most meaningful relationships are designed for the soul's growth. Even the negative ones have something to offer. Have you ever heard someone say, "I married my mother!" If you see yourself in that statement, there's likely an issue you need to work out with mom that you didn't. Now you have drawn to you a partner with a similar personality to help you do just that.

I have heard many people comment on how close they are to their family. On the other hand, there are just as many who are estranged from their kinfolk. It's how we choose to react to our environment that makes or breaks relationships. If we look at our family problems and relationships from a spiritual standpoint, we can gain much insight. Let's say you grew up in an emotionally cold or abusive family. Rather that dwelling on the negative and blaming your parents for everything that's wrong with your life, why not look at the situation and choose to grow from it? Use the experience to understand and help others in similar circumstances. You could become a therapist and help children of abuse. You'd certainly have an understanding of their plight if you grew up in such a challenging environment.

Perhaps in a former lifetime you grew up in a wealthy family and wanted for nothing. In a current lifetime you may be born into poor relations. Your soul may have chosen this path to become less materialistic and gain empathy for those who are less fortunate.

Sometimes a soul has a strong desire to repay a family member for their love and kindness. Let's say in a former lifetime your mother was a "saint," who sacrificed everything for you. In your current lifetime you are repaying the favor, and she is now your child. You feel a strong desire to take care of her.

I know that I had a former lifetime with my father. Then, and in my current incarnation, he was very good to me. When my mother died in this lifetime, I immediately moved back home to live with my dad so he wouldn't be alone. There was nothing to think over. I just did it. It was the right and *only* thing to do. My husband was very upset that I uprooted our family. My business was booming and the kids were happily settled in school. It would have been easier to leave the situation just the way it was and visit my dad on weekends, but I never considered any other alternatives. Moving and dropping everything was what was I supposed to do. I believe it was a promise from one soul to another made eons ago.

Over the course of many different lifetimes, the roles we play in our relationships get reversed. There are givers and takers, teachers and students, parents and children. Sometimes we play the same role over and over, too. It's a repetitive cycle. We also can repeat mistakes and lessons. If there is bad blood between family members, at some point it must be washed away. So if Dad and little Joe don't agree to disagree, they will start a continual pattern, that will follow them from lifetime to lifetime, until one soul acts in a spiritually responsible way and ends the negative cycle. For example, there could be generations of abuse in a family. Until someone works to end the cycle, the indignity will repeat itself not only from generation to generation, but lifetime to lifetime. Roles are often reversed so everyone knows what it feels like to be on the receiving end. The victim becomes the abuser, and the abuser the victim. Trying to right a wrong becomes more difficult with each lifetime.

You reap what you sow.
For every action there is a reaction.
Whatever you put out comes back to you.
Such is the law of karma.

If someone chooses to reincarnate into a specific family to pay back karma or rectify a situation, what about kids who are adopted? These souls may have a very special type of karma, or at the very least, the birth mother does. The child's soul has agreed to be born into one family, but recognizes the birth mother is a tool or vehicle to get into the family he or she is "supposed to be with."

Adoption is no coincidence. Being adopted myself, I know I was destined to be raised by my "dad." Perhaps my birth mother was repaying a debt to my adoptive family by helping them have a child. Many times a couple that can't have children are given the opportunity through another woman. The people may never know one another, but their souls do. Having a child for someone else is one of the most unselfish acts a soul can perform.

Soul Groups

Many people reincarnate in "soul groups." These are the souls born into the same families over many lifetimes. Some souls naturally gravitate towards certain groups of people who have "agreements" to come back together. Many times soul groups are born during a particular period in time or in a generation to learn specific lessons. They may find themselves working together for a unified cause, fighting a war in a specialized unit or even working third shift in a hospital emergency ward. One example of a soul group may be children born right before the Great Depression. These folks needed to be part of that learning experience. What about those that fought in Vietnam? Likely a soul group. And those that died in the tragedy of 9/11? Definitely a soul group.

The people who perished that tragic day sacrificed a longer earthly life to make a statement and teach the world lessons about compassion and spirituality, among other things. Their unselfish act made a difference in the entire world. It was their soul's contract to leave the earth plane at this specific time and be a part of something that would change history and alter life as we know it. Circumstances put their physical bodies at the World Trade Center that fateful day or on one of the hijacked planes. Consciously, they didn't have a clue, but on a soul level they understood what their spiritual mission was. I feel this particular soul group's demise was a contribution to society and may have very well set the stage for the end of terrorism. A contract was made long before they were born into this lifetime, perhaps to be a part of 9/11. No doubt you've heard the story of the man who was supposed to report to work that day at the World Trade Center and decided to go in a little late. Why were some people there and others not? Don't chalk it up to luck or even coincidence. They weren't a part of this particular soul group. But those who were aboard the planes that hit the Twin Towers were.

What about the astronauts who died aboard the space shuttles Columbia and Challenger? The victims and survivors of the Holocaust? The people aboard the Titanic? There are millions of soul groups all over the world working out issues or repaying karmic debt on an unconscious level. What is the lesson or message these souls want to share? Sometimes we get it right away, and sometimes it takes us a little longer to figure it out. But when people perish in tragedies and under bizarre circumstances, especially in groups, understand that their passing may have been part of a large contract between many souls. It was their time to go. Their fate. Their destiny and soul's choice.

Most souls that reincarnate connect with others they felt close to in former lifetimes. Think of all of the families, lovers, and friends that were torn apart over the past hundreds of years, either due to famine, disease, or war. They come back to lovingly reunite or work on unfinished business . . . and some to save the world.

People who belong to a soul group may or may not live their life in the national news headlines. But together, they are working on the same issues or toward a similar goal. They feel a strong bond and need to be together. Usually groups are made up of three or more individuals. They sense a camaraderie of some sort and often come together under unique or unusual circumstances, and some in the strangest of coincidences. They don't necessarily stay together forever. Some are connected through many lifetimes. It is more likely when the mission of the group is completed that the people in the group go their separate ways.

A client of mine named Barbara was fired from her medical job in Atlanta. There was no logical reason for the firing, but there was a spiritual one. She found work in a little Georgia town a few hundred miles away that put her in touch with a small group of dedicated people working on developing a clinic to help homeless people. Barbara took the lower-paying job, feeling this was where she needed to be at the time, and quickly made friends with her co-workers. They were one big, happy family. During a regression session, Barbara reconnected to a previous lifetime in which she and her current co-workers were aiding soldiers in a makeshift hospital during the Civil War. The hospital was set on fire by the Yankees, and many people, including Barbara and her co-workers, lost their lives as they tried to rescue the wounded from the burning infirmary. Their lives cut short, they all were born again into this lifetime to continue where they left off. They all felt a strong urge to complete their mission and a "connection" with one another.

Once the fundraising was complete and the clinic established, new people were hired and the "founders" were slowly weeded out, left to go their own way and off in new directions. Their karma had been completed. The soul group had accomplished what it set out to do. All agreed that their job was finished there.

Past-Life Connections

Almost everyone you meet who plays a significant role in your life or makes a "difference" in some way is likely a past-life connection. A person with whom we have a past-life connection is not necessarily a soul mate. Bonds from previous incarnations are formed with many people over the span of numerous lifetimes. Some of these connections are quite positive, while others are negative. That's why you experience a feeling of déjà vu or familiarity with certain individuals. People come and go in our lives everyday. It's the people who make an impact that we need to take note of.

No relationship that is truly important to us can be "neutral." It's either very positive or very negative. You should warmly embrace all of your past-life connections, whether they be "good" or "bad." Be especially thankful for the challenging ones, because in them you have an opportunity to release heavy karma. Please keep in mind that even if a relationship ends badly, your soul can still learn, grow, and heal from the connection. Perhaps the other person's soul is needing to make a connection for their soul's growth as well. These relationships need not always be intense, but will have an effect on you in some way that changes your life or outlook.

You may have a past-life tie with your grade school teacher who saw great potential in you and encouraged it. It could be that a particular co-worker was instrumental in saving your job. There may be a boss or supervisor whom you despise, for no logical reason.

Past-life connections are not as strong as soul-mate ties, but they are important because they give each of us a chance to reconnect with souls from past lifetimes for a variety of reasons. Sometimes the reason is as simple as missing one another. There are usually lessons associated with these connections, and as we work through the issues presented, some develop into long-term commitments. There are just as many that may be made up of a few fleeting moments that change your perception of life. Let's say a stranger pushed you out of the way of a speeding car. Then your "hero" helped you to your feet and left, never to be seen again. You didn't even get his name! Was he just doing a good deed? What put that particular person in your path, at that very moment? Why him? It was this particular soul's destiny to help save your life. You will never forget his face and kindness. He made a major impact on your life in a matter of mere seconds.

You'll recognize some past-life ties by a feeling of familiarity. It's as if you've met before. You may have strong feelings about a person you know little about. Let's pretend you met someone for the very first time and immediately mistrusted them. You probably had a "bad" experience with this soul in a former existence. They may have lied, cheated, or manipulated you then. Or perhaps it's the other way around, where you immediately like someone from the minute you are introduced. This soul likely played a positive role in another lifetime.

Soul Friends

Soul friends are the dear friends from former lifetimes whom you mingle with in this one. They touch your heart and are there for you through thick and thin. Soul friends talk about everything and share the wildest secrets (the ones you wouldn't dare tell your husband or wife). They celebrate life's joys and sorrows with you. These are your very best friends. Perhaps you haven't seen one another for years, but reunite at some point. You and your soul friend will be able to pick up right where you left off. No amount of time or space diminishes the bond. Youngsters have many soul friends, even imaginary ones. It's all part of the growth process. Think about your best friends. How have they made a difference in your life?

A letter from a pen pal who lives thousands of miles away, a chance meeting at an airport between two people, and coincidental introductions help put soul friends in your path. Sometimes spouses get jealous over these special connections we make with other people. It takes a lot to break apart such a relationship. It stands the test of time, and if a soul friendship does end, both parties feel a sense of great loss and grief just as if there had been a physical death.

The Lovers/Soul-Mate Connection

The topic of soul mates comes up often when I am counseling clients on relationships. Almost everyone asks the question, "When will I meet my soul mate?" I feel the word is used too loosely these days.

Many times when people are in a wonderful relationship, they tend to think they've found their elusive soul mate. People who feel this way describe a deep, soul-stirring emotion. They've been in love before, but nothing like this. They feel no jealousy, no fear, and no threats to the relationship. They feel at peace and complete. Yes, there is a strong possibility they have found a soul mate. But there are many different types of soul mates, and they do not necessarily have to be lovers, spouses, or romantic interests. Yet the majority are. Soul mates come together because they are working on the same type of karma in this lifetime. A soul draws to it what it lacks or needs to complete its mission. On spiritual paths, souls are drawn to one another because they feel a strong connection. Each desires what the other has to fulfill itself and become one. The feeling is not one of infatuation or obsession. It is peace. It is knowing you are supposed to be with a particular person for some higher purpose.

Sometimes you will recognize what this higher purpose is. Other times you will have no clue, but will feel the relationship has a deep spiritual quality to it like no other experienced before. Unconditional love is a good indication of a soul mate. Many times it is possible to determine, through your astrological chart, the presence of a soul mate in your life or when one is coming.

Once you've found your soul mate, it is important to know that you may not choose to be together during this entire lifetime. Yes, legions of soul mates stay together till death do they part, but just as many part ways once their karma is complete. Many people never meet their soul mate. This is not a bad thing. It's just that their soul is choosing to walk its path alone. That is their karma. The most serious of all karmic lessons and unyielding soul "contracts" can be found in our most intimate relationships. This is why our souls desperately seek out past-life connections and soul mates. We're eager to fulfill our lessons, so we must reunite.

Sometimes the vows we take in former lifetimes carry over into our current one. I often use the example of a southern belle seeing her soldier husband off to war in the late 1800s. He tells her to wait for him as he vows to return. She promises to remain forever faithful. But he never comes home. He's killed in battle. Now the southern belle refuses to "move on." Physical death couldn't destroy their love or the vows taken. They are soul mates, and fate will bring them back together one day . . . in another lifetime. Their souls made a promise, which carried over into the next lifetime.

Fast forward one hundred years later, and this southern belle isn't even living down south. She may be a high-ranking executive residing in the Windy City. All of her life she's been searching for something or someone. She's dated but never married. Something's missing. There's a void in her life, and even though she can't explain it, our southern belle knows in her heart that one day she'll find it. She'll meet her soul mate. He'll come back to her.

And he does. She's at a conference and glances at a man across the room. Their eyes meet. It's as if they've known each other forever. The feelings they are both experiencing at that very instant are overwhelming, but they keep their emotions in check. After a two-week, whirlwind courtship, they're engaged and planning a Vegas wedding. She knows and he knows that something very special has happened. They feel complete. They feel as if they've come home.

I have counseled couples who have enjoyed many past lifetimes together. They choose to reunite because of their deep love for one another and cannot fathom living life apart. These are among the folks who have predestined mates. Certain souls make pacts and contracts to reincarnate over many lifetimes and marry each other again and again. If you are single and know in your heart that there is someone special out there but haven't made that special connection with anyone yet, it will happen! If friends and family are urging you to settle down and claim you're just being "too picky," listen only to your heart. When you meet your soul mate, you'll know. The feeling will be different than anything else you've ever experienced before. Your soul has already chosen the right lover for you, so be patient. It will happen when the time is right for you to work on creating or finishing some wonderful karma together.

What about those souls that never seem to fulfill their karma in a relationship? There are millions of couples that constantly fight, argue, and break up, only to get back together again and again. They inflict a lot of emotional pain on one another.

Do you feel like a yo-yo in your relationship? If you don't settle your differences and learn to love one another in this lifetime, you must reincarnate and meet again. You're building negative karma, so the relationship gets more difficult in each and every lifetime. The lessons become harder, too. I've seen people that meet their soul mate, only to find out he or she is involved with or married to someone else. This situation is usually an indication of many former lifetimes together in which the couple refused to work on their problems. Or they have created such heavy karma that they're paying for it in the current incarnation. The duos have to work even harder to be together. These souls are never single at the same time. One is married and the other isn't. Some engage in extramarital affairs.

I never judge anyone because we all have lessons to learn, but my heart goes out to those who become entangled in affairs, because they will have to pay many reparations. The paybacks can be horrendous! I know one client who cheated on her husband with her former high school boyfriend for years. She didn't want to leave her husband, but was still attracted to the ex. "Kim" convinced herself that the cheating was all right because she had been with this man before and both still had strong feelings for one another. What her husband didn't know wouldn't hurt him, or so she thought. But it eventually hurt her. Earlier, I made the statement that whatever you put out comes back to you, sometimes even threefold. About nine years later, Kim was settled happily into her marriage, with a big house, expensive cars, nice vacations, and three beautiful children. She wanted for nothing as her husband was part-owner in a company. Kim was putting all her energy into her marriage at this point and hadn't seen her lover in years. She considered her marriage to be rock-solid. But karma came to call. (It usually does when everything seems to be going just perfectly!) Judgment Day for Kim drew near. Her husband announced he was leaving her and moving out, and she'd have to fend for herself. He was cheating on Kim with a woman at work.

If you're involved with someone who's already married, the best advice I can give you is to step away from the relationship, and let the husband and wife work out their differences or decide to end the marriage. Don't create any negative karma for yourself (even if you think he or she is your soul mate). If the marriage should end, then you know your relationship was meant to be, and you can move forward with a clear conscience.

Kim and her husband have both created karma that they may have to "pay back" when they meet again in another lifetime. Both are still angry with one another and unable to work out their differences. So they'll likely have to repeat and atone for their mistakes. Future circumstances may be even more challenging. There could be trust issues that seem illogical in another lifetime if they meet again.

Have you ever met someone for the first time and immediately didn't like them? Did you feel a mistrust for no reason? As mentioned earlier in the book, whenever you feel a strong like or dislike for someone you first meet, it is likely that this person is from a former lifetime and there was an intense encounter. Your "gut feeling" will be a good indicator as to whether it was a positive or negative relationship. Perpetrators become victims and victims become masters as roles change or reverse, especially in romantic relationships, to settle karmic debts.

Karmic Reasons for Past-Life & Soul-Mate Connections

The Common Reasons Why Soul Mates "Hook Up"

1. To repay a debt.
2. To receive payment of a debt.
3. To right a wrong or learn a lesson.
4. An early death in a former lifetime.
5. For the soul's growth.
6. To complete or finish something.
7. To help another soul.
8. Out of love.

To Repay a Debt

Reparation is one of the main reasons we connect with people from our past. Our souls desperately need to make things right with other souls to whom we owe something. For example, in a former lifetime, Glen was dying on a battlefield in Gettysburg during the Civil War. He was frightened to die alone. Even though there was gunfire blasting all around, another soldier stayed by his side and put his own life in danger as Glen made his "transition." He did not pass on alone. Both soldiers were killed that day.

Now, in his current life, Glen's soul chose to reincarnate into a family that put him in touch with his faithful comrade. His "army buddy" is now his little brother with whom he has a strong bond in this lifetime. The family often remarks on what a wonderful relationship the siblings share. Glen feels a need to help his brother all the time and goes out of his way to repay the karmic debt. Glen's mother remarks how odd it is that when her younger son is sick in bed with the flu or doesn't feel well, he asks for Glen to come and sit in his room or give him his medicine. She admitted she was a little jealous and hurt by not being able to fulfill this nurturing role, but when I explained to her that Glen was just repaying a karmic debt, she didn't feel as "rejected."

Debts can mount over several lifetimes. You can have many smaller notes to pay or a single large bill with interest owed to a particular person. If you made your living as a thief in a past life, you may have to pay all your victims back in this one, or financial troubles could plague you for an entire lifetime. Or, if someone showed kindness to you and touched your former life in a grand manner, you may seek to repay the favor now.

There are no set rules for how long you must make payments or how big the debt actually is. That decision is up to your very own soul. It yearns to make things right and to settle the score in the most positive of ways. You may not even consciously be aware of what you're doing. So if something doesn't seem fair in a relationship or situation, meditate on it. Ask your higher self what it is you are supposed to learn or "pay back." Then be thankful you have the opportunity to do so.

To Receive Payment of a Debt

Sometimes you'll reincarnate and connect with another person so they have the opportunity to pay off a karmic debt to you. You may choose to be part of their life to aid in their soul's growth.

Through regression, my client Mary found out that her current boyfriend had betrayed her in a previous lifetime. She stuck by him through thick and thin, but he had created bad karma in their former lifetime by cheating on her with other women. He was a gambler and often stole her money to try his hand at yet another poker game. When she died, this man finally understood the meaning of love and felt remorse for his actions. He missed her terribly and wanted to atone for these actions. It was too late, at least in that lifetime.

Fast forward one hundred fifty years later, and Mary meets Joe. He feels a strong connection to her and an overwhelming desire to help her that never seems to be fulfilled. Joe wants to help her through whatever crisis she is experiencing. He constantly needs to buy Mary lovely things, often bringing her little gifts for no specific reason. He claims he's never felt such a need to give unselfishly in any other relationship. Meanwhile, Mary is delighted that she's being treated like a queen. However, she doesn't want him to make such a fuss over her, but he insists. Joe is paying back that karmic debt from the couple's former lifetime together. Mary is on the receiving end and should accept his reparations graciously, thus releasing Joe of further debt. Mary deserves all the attention this man gives her, but doesn't fully understand why Joe is so generous, until she goes though her own regression session.

When Mary uncovers this other lifetime of hurt, pain, and betrayal, the pieces of the puzzle all fall into place. Today, Joe's soul feels a need to make amends, and it can't grow until he pays Mary back for the pain he caused.

If someone owes you a debt, you'll eventually figure out who it is because this person has a desperate need to help you. They feel an obligation to go out of their way for you. Many times these relationship debts are found among lovers and family. And remember, if you're in a relationship and treating someone poorly, you'll have to suffer the consequences of your actions sooner or later. Mary collected on her debt, and the slate was wiped clean. Even though her soul didn't have to come back and reconnect with Joe, she chose to do so for his soul growth and gave him the opportunity to "pay in full."

To Learn a Lesson or Right a Wrong

Have you ever been in a relationship that you just couldn't "get right"? No matter how hard you work on it, the two of you are always in turmoil, constantly breaking up and making up. You desperately want to be together, yet both of you may be stubborn people who can't even agree to disagree. In many situations, egos get in the way. But if you don't work out your problems in this lifetime, you must in the next, and often the lessons of the heart are much harder later on.

I know a couple that were never single at the same time but wanted to be together. They were definitely soul mates with a history of many lifetimes together. Chris was married while Sam was single. Sam got tired of waiting for her to leave her husband, and walked down the aisle with someone else. A year later Chris got divorced and waited around a few years for Sam to do the same. He didn't file. Then Chris met someone new, and half-heartedly married a second time. Meanwhile, Sam stayed committed to his wife for twenty years until she died of cancer. Chris consoled him but wouldn't leave her marriage "because of the kids." She promised they'd be together in a few years down the road. Another woman pursued Sam and moved into his house. Now in a panic and not wanting to endure this repetitive cycle, Chris is seriously thinking of ending her marriage. At fifty years old, she is scared to give up the security she enjoys but knows she's supposed to be with Sam.

Whew! What a soap opera. This is an obvious example of two people who know they are soul mates but must contend with difficult lessons. Their paths cross at all the wrong times, but they never let go of the dream of being together one day. Impatience, jealousy, and insecurity drive them to make commitments to others they don't really love. Will they ever get together in this lifetime? Only if one of them remains single long enough and sacrifices other relationship opportunities, is patient, and willing to wait. There is a happy ending to this story. Chris and Sam finally did get married, but what struggles they went through!

I know a few of you can identify with Chris and Sam. If you have a similar story to tell, know that you will be together at some point, but your souls must be strong and patient. If not in this lifetime, you will be united with your soul mate in the next one. This type of a test creates a stronger and more determined bond between souls because they must learn what they are missing. They have to feel the pain and frustration of not being together to appreciate one another in the next lifetime.

Chris and Sam's relationship was, among other things, about learning to trust their hearts. It's probable that they have tried to work on this exact same issue in former lifetimes.

So what are Chris and Sam's other lessons? Patience. Trust. Agreeing to work things through. Not allowing the ego and selfishness to destroy such a connection. Did you catch what else happened in this scenario? Chris and Sam both created more karma by rushing into marriage with other souls for the wrong reasons.

The only way to complete this karmic task was for the couple to work through their differences, recognize how important the relationship is to both of them, and make a solid commitment.

Some of the challenges we experience on life's path may actually be blessings, for they give us the opportunity to grow as a soul. Some of your most difficult life lessons will make you a stronger person.

To Help Someone Along Their Path

There are some souls that don't need to reincarnate. They've reached a level of enlightenment where they aren't required to revisit the earth plane but choose to do so to help others on their path. Some souls purposely place themselves in positions where they can do the most good for mankind or a single being.

Gloria is such a soul. Just being around her, one feels a sense of peace. She is gentle, soft-spoken, and wise. Her mission in this lifetime was to help a special man develop a spiritual center. The problem was this man she was to assist wasn't very spiritual. In fact, he drank too much and was rather self-centered, and money was his god. Under unusual circumstances they met while both were traveling abroad. They were immediately attracted to one another and later married. This gentleman was guided by his new wife's vision. By using his business skills, he started a cable television show in his area promoting speakers and authors. Gloria suggested that he book self-help and spiritual writer as guests. When he did, the ratings went through the roof! A short time later, the couple were drawing thousands of viewers, and lots of people wanted to get on their show.

Gloria kept nudging her husband to do even more to enlighten their local community. Within a few years, a spiritual retreat center was built, and people from all over the world came to visit, attend seminars, and discover ways to improve their own lives.

Gloria's husband says he can't believe how his life has changed and how he views the world and the collective consciousness. By helping one man develop a spiritual path, Gloria has opened the door for a million more souls to find peace and growth in their own lives.

Gloria's story is not unique. There are many more like hers. There are humble stories, too, involving just one or two people. Sometimes a person will devote their entire life to another; perhaps a lover or a child. The recipient's life is drastically changed because of this soul's influence. An example of this would be a soul incarnating to be the mother of a child with a disability. The child needs help on their path. We could turn this around and suggest the child is helping the mother, too. A soul comes back in an uncomfortable body, giving the mother the opportunity to grow spiritually and develop empathy and compassion through devoting her life to this child who needs her so much.

Separation Because of an Early Death in a Former Lifetime

Another type of connection is when a person's life is cut short by an untimely death and their loved one is left behind with a broken heart. The loved one can't release the person or the pain. It's unfortunate, but many times the bereaved person refuses to go on with life and gets stuck in a time warp. The pain of the loss runs so deep that it causes a fixed, unyielding nature. Some people are unable to love again, or they take a vow never to love again. When reincarnation occurs, the souls are drawn by this unique energy and feel a strong desire to be reunited. I have seen this in the case of mother and child just as much as with husband and wife.

The problem that occurs in the current lifetime is one partner is so frightened and paranoid their partner will leave them that they smother the person or live in constant fear that something bad is going to happen in the relationship. Most of the time their fears are unfounded. These subconscious fears are brought over from a former lifetime. They are the memories our souls maintain. Perhaps some are images of our past-life joys, lessons, and tears. Even though our conscious mind is wiped clean of the prior existence when we are born again, our soul still possesses imprints of that existence. If left ignored and misunderstood, these past-life memories haunt us and our new relationships. Unfortunately, some people center their entire lives around these fears. Or, not wanting to experience the pain of loss, people refuse to make emotional commitments in relationships. But there is hope. Some people can be helped through past-life regression counseling and meditation.

When this specific karmic past occurs in a mother/child relationship, mom can be overly protective to the point that it's not healthy for the youngster. In a romantic relationship, we see signs of insecurity, jealousy, and unfounded phobias.

These phobias do make sense, though, if you look at them from a past-life point of view. There have been millions of people over the past hundreds of years whose lives were torn apart because of war, famine, and the like. Families were ripped apart. People died unexpectedly every day because of accidents and senseless murders. Because loved ones never got a chance to say goodbye or finish their karma with others, the deceased souls felt cheated. Those that passed away are anxious to get back to earth to reunite with loved ones left behind.

If you're involved in a relationship where you have unfounded fears or are overly vigilant about your partner's basic security, you may be dealing with a past-life issue. It would be worth investigating, to eliminate the fear and enjoy living in the present. In most cases, if you cannot trace a fear or phobia back to your childhood years or events that have occurred in your current incarnation, you are very likely dealing with an issue brought over from another lifetime. These issues can be eradicated by getting help from a professional past-life therapist.

Unfinished Business

You've probably heard the phrase "I have unfinished business with him!" Souls have unfinished business, too. In many past lives, lessons were not learned, tasks were left undone, and relationships were not consummated. The unfinished business can be a positive or negative thing, but a lot of times it is negative. A soul feels a strong need to complete something.

Such was the case with my client Sharon. She and her boyfriend were together for six years before they decided to tie the knot, but only after much indecisiveness on her part. Their relationship was abusive. She was a battered woman who always returned to the relationship after the beatings. The couple was in therapy for years. One day she called for another session with me and asked for the hundredth time, "What should I do?" The patterns between these folks were so repetitive.

Wedding dates were planned and canceled several times. No matter what I told her, Sharon always went back to him. There was no logic to this. In the past I had told her to break it off and move on, but she never did. When I started looking at this relationship from a karmic standpoint, I told her something drastically different. Most people would have scolded me for such a thing, but I told her go ahead and get married. I also told Sharon she would be divorced in less than two years, and her longing for this man would then end. She would no longer have any feelings for him. It's something that her soul had to finish. Sharon had to get married to break the bond.

We did a past-life session and uncovered some amazing information, which we'll get to later. Sharon set a date, and the couple married on an exotic island. The wedding pictures were beautiful, but as soon as the "I do's" were said, the fights started. Sharon threw up in the limo because she was drunk. Her groom got drunk and flirted with other women on their honeymoon. When the couple returned home, they built an expensive home, but within nine months were headed for divorce court. Sharon was okay with it. The divorce went through, and Sharon never went back. I feel it's truly over. She does, too. Her soul had accomplished what it needed to do. It was set free.

This past-life regression session proved that she had unfinished business with her ex-husband. The two of them had been engaged in a former lifetime, but secretly. Her parents wouldn't allow the union. She promised him she would find a way to marry him, but it was not to be back then. Relatives made sure they were kept apart; and years later Sharon looked for her lover but found he had passed on. Her vow to marry him would have to be fulfilled, if not in that lifetime, then in a later one. She finished her business two hundred years later in the year 2001. His abusive nature is another issue. Was he still angry at Sharon for not trying harder to be with him in that prior lifetime? Was he scared of losing her all over again, so he tried to lower her self-esteem to keep her in the marriage? That may be why he tried to keep her away from her friends and family in this lifetime, too, so they couldn't influence her decision to marry him now. Sharon's family was not happy with him in this lifetime either.

Perhaps there is something you feel a drive to accomplish. No one understands why you feel so passionately about this cause, but you do. For example, a young white lawyer I counseled named Jeff is heavily involved in human rights. He has managed his career so that he is in a position to change some laws to benefit the African American community. He spends a lot of his free time organizing youth activities and supporting education in poverty-stricken neighborhoods. Growing up in an affluent white neighborhood, Jeff never had much exposure to other cultures until he turned fourteen and his parents divorced. He went to live with his mother in low-income housing in a diverse neighborhood.

During one of our regression sessions, Jeff saw himself living in the old South, somewhere in Georgia, putting together the Underground Railroad that helped slaves seeking freedom move to the North. He had just started developing new escape routes for the slaves when authorities discovered what he was doing and Jeff was sent to prison. He felt he had never completed his mission. Fast forward one hundred fifty years later, and Jeff is completing what his soul set out to do back in the Civil War days. He's helping a certain sector of society improve their quality of life.

Oftentimes we have unfinished business in our relationships. If you feel you need to end something or find closure with a situation or person, there's likely some door that was never shut tight. It's good to finish up and move on. Otherwise this business may hold you back from progressing in other areas of your life. You may be so obsessed with one subject that you can't focus on anything else in your life. It's more than just passion. It's more like obsession. You must complete it.

For the Soul's Growth

Yet another reason we choose to reincarnate is simply for our soul's growth. As we move through each lifetime, we learn new lessons, accomplish tasks, develop talents, and advance to higher levels of spiritual enlightenment. You can think of soul advancement like this: You're in spiritual study from kindergarten through college. There are different classes, teachers, and tests in all the grades. Your soul chooses what it yearns and needs to learn. As the soul grows, it becomes closer to God, which is where it longs to be. Sometimes you may get stuck in first grade and need to take another course in compassion. Perhaps a soul isn't happy with an average grade in empathy and chooses to hold itself back to really grasp the knowledge it needs to get an A+.

Most of our soul's growth comes through our dealings in our most personal relationships. It is through difficulty, sorrow, tragedy, and pain that we learn the most and experience the most growth. Many of us recall happy, joy-filled times, but just as many fade from memory. However, we never forget the crises we live through. They change us in deep, profound ways. If your life seems to be filled with crisis after crisis, know that when you handle challenges, from a spiritual standpoint your soul is advancing to yet another level. Accept these karmic lessons as opportunities for your soul to become enlightened and closer to God.

Out of Love

Many souls make pacts with those they love to reincarnate back to-gether just because their love is so strong and intense. They can't stand the thought of being without one another and often will con-tinue to marry in each and every lifetime. A love like this is so pow-erful that the energy it creates holds people together for lifetimes.

Then there's the mother/child bond. It's so strong that it can transcend several lifetimes as well. A mother's love is perhaps the strongest of any because it's unconditional. Many mothers want to be reunited with their children because they love them so much. If a soul has such a need, it will find a way to get back to earth to be a part of the children's lives, though perhaps playing a different role.

Linda was fifty-two when she died and left four teenagers be-hind. She was a devoted mom and was angry with the illness that ripped her away from her family. Her daughter Sherri came to see me one day, pregnant and due on Linda's birthday. "I feel my mother is with me," she said. "I sense her all around." Little did she know how true that statement was.

When the baby boy was born, he had the eyes of an old soul. Sherri started having strange dreams immediately in which her mother would come to her and reassure her she hadn't died and that she was now reunited with the family. The baby's cry would al-ways wake Sherri up. As time went on and her little boy turned four, he started telling Sherri about relatives he had never met. Sherri was startled that he knew so much about so many personal things in the family. I told her to ask her boy about his "other life." Kids still retain memories of their most previous lifetimes before they are four or five. By the school years, they lose that memory, so it was important that Sherri ask him now. She did, and called me right away with news. "He said he knew me in a former lifetime, but I wasn't his mom. He said he took care of me!" Sherri confided. Did Sherri's mother come back? Was she born into the family she so desperately didn't want to leave? There is no real proof, only theories, but it was enough for Sherri to recognize she and her son have a very special bond.

There's' something else at work here, too . . . and we call it karma.

Karma

There are so many definitions of karma, many of which are quite confusing. Simply put, whatever you put out comes back to you. For every action, there is a reaction. Whatever kindness you do will come back to you threefold. Likewise, any negative deeds will also come back at you.

Karma teaches us lessons. If you fail or refuse to learn your lessons, they will keep coming back until you do. The purpose of karma is to move our souls to a higher level. The more we learn, the more we grow. When our ego takes over and we refuse to learn, karma doles out more lessons, and sometimes they become harder to learn.

It is important to remember that you are the only person responsible for your karma. It is the result of your own thoughts and deeds, not someone else's. If a person has unfinished business (karma) when they die, their soul still needs to fulfill its karma, or it can't advance to the next level of spiritual enlightenment. Therefore, when it reincarnates into the next lifetime, it still has to deal with the karma from the previous lifetime. That is why we meet so many people with similar problems and seem to deal with the same issues over and over again. Does the same scenario continue to pop up in your relationships? Are the patterns similar with everyone you are intimate with? I feel that anyone you have a strong bond with in this lifetime or have major issues with is part of your karma from a past life.

Sometimes when you first meet a person, you know right away there's some sort of connection between the two of you. With others, it may take a few "lessons" to figure it out. Remember, karma can be good or bad. It can carry over from several lifetimes. It is easier to deal with karma in your current lifetime, but with each lifetime this unfinished business becomes harder and harder to complete.

I have helped many people identify what their karma is over the years. I've also been able to pinpoint exact people with whom they have past-life or soul connections through their astrological charts. Here's an example of good karma concerning two "soul friends."

The New Orleans Nuns

Cindy and Angie had a strong past-life connection. Both being spiritually open to such ideals, they shared their feelings and beliefs with one another. When they first met in 1993, they felt an instant recognition and talked like old friends. They both had a desire to find out where this connection came from. After a few meditation and past-life regression sessions, the friends were able to narrow down the past life they had shared. Both were Ursuline nuns who had been assigned to come over from France to New Orleans in the early 1800s. This would explain Cindy's attraction to the historic French Quarter in this lifetime. She also has no desire to visit the former Ursuline Convent in the Quarter when she visits. She claims her stomach gets upset just crossing the street on which it sits.

Back then, nuns were brought over from France to educate and bring religion to the city, which was infested with greed, gambling, piracy, and other goings-on. Every time Cindy visits New Orleans, she has terribly vivid dreams depicting life a century or so ago. Many people she knows today show up in these dreams. She has often shared these dreams with me, and they are very descriptive. It seems that by being in New Orleans, her subconscious is opening itself up to another time in which she lived. This must have been a significant lifetime for her because she remembers names, faces, and buildings. Some of the sites she describes can still be found in the Quarter today.

After doing more research and meditation, Cindy and Angie agreed that they had been very close friends. During this prior lifetime, Cindy had fallen sick from the yellow-fever epidemic. Angie had been at Cindy's deathbed around the clock. She was taking care of her during her final days and helping guide her into the afterlife. Cindy made a promise then. She vowed that she would be with Angie to help her through her transition in the next lifetime.

This came to pass. Shortly after they met in 1993, Angie was dying of breast cancer. Families and friends had been there every day for six months as her conditioned worsened. Out of the blue, Cindy left her own family and quit her job to come sit at Angie's bedside. She was there twenty-four hours a day, seven days a week, nursing her and talking with her.

Family came in and out, but Cindy stayed. Three weeks later, Angie was ready to leave the earth plane. Cindy was right there, holding Angie's hand as she took her final breath . . . just as she had promised to do in the lifetime they had shared more than one hundred fifty years earlier.

Angie laid good karma in the New Orleans lifetime by helping her friend on her final journey. Cindy repaid that karmic debt by doing the same lifetimes later. To this day, Cindy says she doesn't really know why she chose to drop everything and take care of Angie even though Angie had nurses and family there for her. She said it was just the right thing to do. "It was just natural. I knew I was the one who was supposed to be there. It was something I had to do. Nothing else in the world mattered," she recalled.

These two friends recognized their connection early on in their relationship, but they didn't recognize what their karma was or what debt was to be paid until the end of the relationship.

Repetitive Patterns

Mickey and Sharly share a different story. Their karma is not easy to define. No matter how hard they try to work out issues or end their turbulent relationship, it doesn't happen. During a past-life session, we were able to discover that Mickey was in love with Sharly, who had the talent to make it big in the music industry as a singer.

But Mickey wanted to control Sharly and was jealous of any success that might take her away from him. The two became co-dependent on one another. Their lifestyle contributed to their drug and alcohol abuse. Sharly eventually died of an overdose, never realizing her dream of becoming famous. Mickey never married and for years after Sharly's death was a recluse.

In this lifetime, these two met and instantly fell in love. The attraction was so great and so intense that they both felt it and became inseparable. On their first date they started arguing over silly little things and fell into co-dependent patterns like you would expect to see in a long-term marriage.

Ironically, both of these individuals had an interest in acting and singing in this lifetime. They both felt they would have to accomplish their individual goals before they could marry, and worked hard on their careers. During the course of their relationship, they were constantly breaking up and getting back together. Sharly always felt something holding her back from trusting Mickey. She couldn't explain it. She had never loved anyone so strongly before, but she knew the relationship wasn't good for her. She also was angry with Mickey for reasons she could not explain.

On numerous occasions, she had cheated on him or lied to him. When she did these things, she always felt vindicated. These two kept repeating the same cycle over and over for the next few years. Finally Sharly came to me for past-life counseling sessions. We started the long, hard journey of releasing her karma from the previous lifetime so she could get on with this one. These two had heavy karma to deal with. I was sure they had experienced many similar lifetimes together before. In each lifetime the problem persisted and grew stronger. Obsession, control, and anger were evident. Somewhere in their subconscious, these two knew they had to make this relationship right, to turn it around and make positive choices. That was why it was so difficult to end the relationship for good. Because they weren't aware of what really lay behind the current conditions, they grew frustrated. Bad karma followed more bad karma as the couple continued hurting each other.

The reason Sharly didn't leave was that she couldn't until they finished that old karma or released it. Both felt compelled to stay together. They had debts to pay to each other. So Mickey continued to hurt Sharly, and Sharly, in turn, hurt Mickey, and the karma went back and forth. Thus, there was no end in sight.

Once people like Mickey and Sharly are enlightened about the law of karma, they can repay their debts and release them.

Releasing Karmic Debts

When someone is spiritually enlightened, he or she does not have to be a keeper of bad karma forever. The chain needs to be broken at some point. Look at the previous story between Mickey and Sharly. It was Sharly who was the "victim" in the previous lifetime. Mickey had given her drugs and had taken control of her life, thus leading to her demise.

Sharly doesn't know why she feels anger toward Mickey, even though she loves him so much, but at times she wants to hurt him. It's as if she feels he deserves it.

When such a feeling comes over Sharly, she can stop herself and ask, "Why?" She needs to examine her real motivation for hurting him. She can make a conscious decision to stop "trying to get back at him." If she can do this every time she feels the urge to use or hurt him, she is saying no to karmic retribution, thus breaking patterns set over lifetimes. She is also avoiding retribution now and in future lifetimes. This is not always easy to do, especially if we are working on the ego level.

Now let's look at it from Mickey's point of view. Sharly doesn't believe in karma in this current lifetime, but Mickey does. Mickey understands the pain he put Sharly through in a former life. He may even accept and acknowledge it.

Once Mickey accepts the debt and holds no resentment for Sharly's current anger, he can forgive her. He will not fight back, but will do all he can to bring peace to the situation. Mickey is handling his karmic responsibilities correctly. In the next lifetime the pattern will not be repeated, and it's likely the karmic debt will be paid in full.

There is another technique I have discovered in the past several years for releasing karma from prior lifetimes, called "3 in 1 Concepts." It is a form of therapy that gets right to the root of problems and is emerging as a great tool in helping people with all sorts of issues, not just those from prior lifetimes, but current conditions as well. Facilitators of this type of therapy, using suggested remedies such as flower essences, affirmations, balancing, and color therapy, make corrections to the client's subconscious, conscious, and emotional states in current times. Negative energies and thoughts are then released, and in turn some karmic patterns are immediately halted.

Each time we are born into a new lifetime, our soul still retains a "memory" of our previous incarnation, but our conscious mind does not. Therefore experiences, fears, talents, traumas, and the like are engraved in our genetic cells and our subconscious mind. By using age-recession and generation-recession techniques, clients can be gently guided back to the thoughts and emotions of a prior lifetime.

Perhaps the worst thing about karmic debt is that we don't remember what it is we are paying for. Whatever our debt was that we brought over from a previous reincarnation, we have no conscious memory of it.

Therefore, past-life regression, meditation, astrological study, and spiritual awareness are essential in breaking, healing, and making restitution for the karmic debts from our past.

Karmic Paybacks

We all make karmic repayments every day. You need to be aware and accepting of this. Let's say something negative happens to you at work. You should stop and think, "What did I do recently to deserve this? Did I mistreat someone yesterday, a week ago, a year ago?" Whatever you put out comes back to you. Even thoughts are like boomerangs. Put out a negative thought, and you'll get it back. If you think you can achieve something, you will. If you wake up in the morning and say, "I just know it's going to a rotten day," the prediction will probably hold true.

However you want to be treated is how you must treat others. If you want to be understood, you must listen. If you want respect, you must give it. If you want love, you must open your heart to it. People born under the sign of Scorpio have a very special type of karma, called Kash-Karma. Kash-Karma brings immediate paybacks for good or bad deeds in this lifetime. This sign doesn't necessarily have to wait until another lifetime to get theirs!

I'll never forget my best buddy Dan from high school, a Scorpio. I consider him a soul friend. He was such a character. When we were about eighteen years old, he invited me to a very nice dinner one evening. When the bill came, he told me to go ahead to the ladies room and he'd meet me in the outside lobby. I did and found him with an anxious look on his face. "C'mon," he whispered, "let's get out of here." I ran after him questioning his rush.

"I'll tell you in the car," he said. As he wheeled out of the parking lot, he was laughing. "I skipped out on the bill!" he said. "We got a free dinner!" We only drove about two miles when we saw a police officer sitting on the side of the road. He immediately pulled us over. The officer said Dan was speeding thirty miles over the speed limit. We both knew he wasn't. He was promptly handed a ticket by the officer who told him he could fight it in court. Our $70 dinner was ruined.

The court date was set for Dan to challenge the ticket. I was to be a witness for Dan. We went, we lost, and Dan had to pay the fine of, yes, $70! Even though I was an unknowing accomplice in Dan's plan, it so happened the court date was set on my birthday and I had to spend the entire day in a small county courthouse, waiting for our turn to be heard. To make matters worse, I took the day off from work without pay. All of this would not have happened if we had just paid the dinner bill.

This is an example of the way the universe works in paying us back the karma we owe. If you think you're getting away with something, you'll end up paying in the long run! Just think of all of the people who seem to be getting away with things. There are those people who think they will never get caught. Karma will catch up to them sooner or later, and their paybacks will be something else!

I also remember when I had my purse stolen in a locker room years ago. I was devastated. I had just cashed my payroll check. All the money for the next few weeks was in the purse, plus a 35mm camera and, of course, all of my identification. The police were called and said there was nothing they could do. "How could this happen to such a nice person like me?" I moaned. "What did I do to deserve this?" I hadn't ripped anyone off. Almost a week later, I received a raise at work, I got free tickets to a sold-out concert, and I won a weeklong trip to Tennessee. I was rewarded karmically threefold by the universe for what had been taken from me. I have often wondered what happened to the purse thieves!

Recently, a friend who owns a retail store was at another department store. She took five dresses up to the cashier. The cashier forgot to ring one up, so my friend didn't say anything and figured she had gotten a free dress. A week later one of her customers used a stolen credit card. The fraud cost her $240. The dress she got for "free" was only $39.95. She learned an expensive karmic lesson!

Paying off Karmic Debt

You can pay off your debt if you know what your karma is. If the same problems and situations keep coming up in your life, you should have a pretty good indication of what your karma is. If you need more help, you can do some past-life regression work, but there probably is a central theme running in your life right now. Stop and take some time to consider what it is, or whom it is with. Maybe you have a few karmic debts. Some of you may have many to pay. (You have my sympathy.) But hey, look at it this way: if it seems as if your karmic note is as big as the national debt, then it's a good thing. Why? Because you're getting the debt paid off now and won't have to deal with these issues or people in another lifetime. But that's only if you agree to handle your liability in a responsible way now. So work it off, sweetheart!

Because I'm a Cancer, a sign that astrologically rules home, family, and children, women who are desperate to have children are drawn to me for readings. In some cases their doctors have given them little or no hope of ever conceiving. They usually don't get pregnant no matter how hard they try. Even in-vitro fertilization doesn't work in some of these cases. In these situations, I always look to the astrological chart of the individual and their mate to see where the karmic responsibility lies. More than likely, the present conditions have to do with a past lifetime of not wanting children or being neglectful to the ones they did have. Since the couple have no recollection of such a past life, they can't understand why such good, loving people shouldn't be blessed with children.

Often if the woman or man performs some sort of service to children in the current lifetime, such as working with abused kids or even adopting them, the karma is paid back and they then will conceive. How many times have you heard that as soon as a woman adopts a child, she becomes pregnant? It happens all the time. This is a good example of balancing your karma.

I must add that in just as many cases a woman's astrological chart will show that she will indeed have children and often how many, though sometimes it is not a couple's destiny. Perhaps they already learned the lesson of parenting in a former lifetime and do not need to go through these steps again. However, I do find aspects that indicate a couple will not have children or will have conception problems in charts of people who have no desire to have a family.

Here's another way of looking at karmic debt being repaid in a current lifetime. Many people are born with disabilities or experience health problems. Many bring these issues over from a former lifetime. A man from Michigan had a previous lifetime in which he was a soldier and was killed in war. During a past-life regression session, he saw himself in uniform, something like that of a Union soldier in the Civil War. He knew he didn't want to fight. He was forced to join the army and was killed in battle. In this lifetime, he reincarnated with a health problem that made him ineligible for any kind of military service.

The health problems came up around his eighteenth birthday. His soul made sure he wouldn't be eligible for any draft in this lifetime. It's amazing that the illness uncovered was related to the area of the body in which he was shot in the war in the previous lifetime. During a regression he saw himself being shot in the head, and in this lifetime he was diagnosed with a mental illness. He paid his karma in that other lifetime—he paid back a debt by giving his life. So in this lifetime he is being rewarded. Rewarded? Yes.

He will never have to fight in a war, and he is still able to live a comfortable lifestyle. His illness is under control with medication, and all of his needs are taken care of.

On a similar note, many people wonder why babies are born with defects or why anyone would want to be born blind or crippled. These souls could be choosing to atone for their past actions in another lifetime. Their souls have chosen this path and are more than accepting. Sometimes people with disabilities do not have to atone for their actions from a previous lifetime, but choose their current situation to help bring understanding to their families or friends for their souls' growth.

I will never forget as long as I live the devastating and true story my father told me one day. When he was a young boy, there had been a neighbor boy who was quite mischievous. The boy was walking in the woods one day and caught a crow. He took out his pocket knife and cut the crow's eyes out. He let the crow go, wandering blindly, living the rest of its days in the dark woods. The boy bragged about what he had done for weeks afterwards.

I thought this was the cruelest and most inhumane act I had ever heard of. But the story is not over. When the young boy grew up, he married and was expecting a child. When the baby finally arrived, it was born without eyes. There were holes in the eye sockets. That story made an impact on me and to this day sends chills up my spine.

This a perfect example of an unselfish soul coming down from heaven to teach its father a lesson and possibly pay back the karma for the father. It took years for the karma to come back, but when it did it, it hit hard.

There is a reason for everything. God's plan is grand. Ultimately, our goal is for all our souls' paths to reach the highest level of spiritual enlightenment that we possibly can. Then what do we make of murderers, con artists, child molesters, and people who rape and steal? Why do they do what they do? All of us are on a journey to get to that highest spiritual place. The choices we make allow some of us to reach that level sooner than others.

God has given us the power of free will, the power to make our own choices. Some choices are obviously better than others. Many times the younger souls do not have a good understanding of what is expected of them and how to relate to others. The younger the soul, the more lessons there are to learn. Sometimes the lessons are much harder than those that older souls choose to deal with.

Some older souls don't always have to reincarnate. They have already reached a certain level of understanding and enlightenment, so it's really not necessary. But those who do choose to come back are often here for a higher purpose. Among them you will recognize your spiritual leaders, researchers, teachers, and healers. Many are found living their lives in humble service to others. They seem to never complain. That's because they know exactly what they are meant to do with their lives. Sometimes they come back just to help younger souls on their journey. The loss of a child at an early age can sometimes be explained under this theory.

I remember a client of mine who had two children, an eight-year-old daughter and a fifteen-year-old son. The brother and sister were extremely close. They loved one another more than most siblings, and the boy always did things with his younger sister. He never fussed if she wanted to hang out with him all the time.

He died one day in a terrible accident. His grief-stricken mother came to see me, and could not understand why this had happened, why her son's life had been cut short. After heavy meditation and prayer, I was able to understand and express exactly what had happened. I knew the message I received was the right one. I cried along with this mother as I expressed what spirit had allowed me to feel.

The son has finished his karma or lesson here on earth. The soul agreement between the brother and sister was simple: he was to help her feel safe and secure in her early years while their parents were going through a divorce. By doing this, it helped him achieve his purpose, which was to learn to love. His sister was the vehicle for this. After he had learned to love so unselfishly, he was to return home. That was agreed upon before they both came over in the current incarnation. His lesson was over.

The mother and I accepted this message because it felt so right. We both knew that we had received a special gift of "knowing" from God. The little sister told her mother that after her brother's death, he often spoke to her. She would hear his voice at times. Their bond had still not been broken.

Children, unlike most adults, do have a strong connection to the "other side." Their minds have not been filled with suspicions or negativity, like adults. Therefore, they are open to feeling the vibrations of loved ones who have passed on. Children, especially those under the age of seven, have not turned over that special intuitive and spiritual side they possess to the mundane world. Thus they have the ability to communicate more easily with the souls of those they love. That's why so many children tell their parents, "I saw grandpa last night," or "Aunt Betty came to say hello." Adults pass this off as the workings of an overactive imagination. Most children are not lying when they express these coincidences, and should not feel afraid to do so.

Past-life regression and meditation can be helpful in order to understand how to work on issues of loss and sadness. Trusting your own heart is always the way to go. All of us are intuitive beings. The more we trust our inner feelings, the more they will work for us, to help us. You can call this a mother's intuition, a gut feeling, or psychic ability. Whatever you call it, it works. Sometimes you'll know who is calling when the telephone rings. Sometimes you'll be at the right place at the right time for a job offer.

Trust your intuition. It won't fail you. Trust your feelings about someone. Your soul won't deceive you. Your head may play games with your heart, but your soul doesn't lie. If you know something to be true, you will experience overwhelming emotion. If you meet a stranger who seems like a dear old friend, this is truth. If you are so mesmerized by a beautiful sunset that it brings tears to your eyes, this is truth. Anything or anyone that affects you in such a strong, positive, powerful way is truth.

Truth gives positive energy to our emotions. Someone who triggers these emotions in your heart may just turn out to be a soul mate. In this next true account, you'll see how a simple dream helped two soul mates recognize one another. But don't ignore the fact that the connection had already been made in their subconscious minds.

A Soul-Stirring Experience

I recall a client from New York who had an interesting experience when she discovered her soul mate. For months, June had been having the same dreams at night. In the dreams, she always met a particular man in a strange bar. She described this man in great detail—what he was wearing, his mannerisms, his eyes. She told me she felt as if her dream was trying to tell her something. When she was on a business trip out of state, she went into a bar, and before her stood this man who had been in her dreams!

She was speechless. She felt a strong connection to this man. She remembered his eyes (the eyes are the windows of the soul). What did this mean? Was this her soul mate? The man also was from out of town and came into the bar lost and looking for help with directions. When he saw June, his mouth dropped. He told her he had been having dreams about her over the past few weeks. Before the evening was over, June dropped her boyfriend of two years, and the new couple made plans to move in together and get married. The relationship was very intense.

Everything just fell into place. I do not know what happened to June and her soul mate. I haven't heard from her since. But a meeting such as theirs only happens once in a lifetime, if at all. Their dreams were definitely their subconscious alerting them to the fact that they were about to have a powerful encounter. The dreams helped them recognize each other so their souls would be guaranteed a chance to come together.

If you find your soul mate in this lifetime, it is important to find out what it is you are meant to be working on together. The relationship will fall in place pretty easily if you are aware of these responsibilities. Many times soul mates become marriage partners. But just as many people, if not more, don't marry their soul mate. This shouldn't be shocking news. Just look at the divorce rate in the country today! I feel there are more couples in what I call a "karmic marriage" than in a soul-mate relationship. Read on to see if you or someone you know can relate.

The "Karmic Marriage"

When you agree to marry someone, you are also saying "I do" to their karmic lessons. You agree to take on their karmic debt. Let's say you lived a wonderful life and had a nice home, a great job, lots of extra cash, and no worries. If you were to marry someone who had ten ex-spouses, lots of child-support payments, no job, and terrible credit, then by marrying that person you would be taking on their issues, their debts, their troubles, problems, baggage, and their *karma!*

Many times, these types of marriages are frustrating and difficult. If the husband and wife choose to build a loving home environment, they are building good karma. Many of these unions offer souls a way to balance out karma from other lifetimes. Usually it is not good karma. There could have been previous betrayal, neglect, rape, and even murder.

By the two building a solid, nurturing home and sometimes a family together, they are repaying the debt from a previous lifetime. These types of marriages are often the ones that are wrought with difficulty and disappointment, but that eventually lead to fulfillment.

If you're in a karmic marriage, you feel as if you can't leave even when things are at the very worst. Friends and family can't believe you won't leave and probably even tell you that you should. But for some reason, you can't. You don't really know why it's so hard to leave the marriage, but in your heart and soul you feel an obligation. You're supposed to stay. Your soul needs to stay to work something out. You will hear many couples say, "We've made it through hell and back." After all they've been through, they've earned good karma. Then they will experience the good life—a nice family, a dream home, more money, and good times. We all know marriage is hard work. A karmic marriage is the soul's work.

And just as in all past-life, karmic, and soul-mate connections, there is always a "theme" or a grand lesson for the couple to work on. This next chapter will give you more insight into what your specific lesson may be in your marriage or committed relationship.

Is Your Marriage Blessed or Cursed?
Discovering Your Love Lesson Through Numerology

Special Note: I use the word marriage in this section to describe a committed union. However, not all "marriages" are legal ones. If you've been in a long-term relationship, lived with someone, or had children together, this may also constitute a marriage.

What Am I Supposed to Learn from Love?

There's a lesson to learn in every relationship. Those you've walked away from may have given you a new perspective on love. If you've been dumped, you've learned the hard way. If you're a person who hangs in there when the going gets tough, it may be due to an overwhelming sense of guilt or responsibility. Most of the time our heaviest karma involves those with whom we march down the aisle. The day we exchange "I do's" can set the tone for an entire lifetime if we choose to stay together until death do us part.

All marriages experience some sort of challenge just as they do joy. There's a "higher reason" you've chosen to settle down with a specific person. This reason usually has to do with a lesson that your souls, together, need to learn.

Here's a numerology formula designed for those couples who are still trying to figure out what it is they're supposed to learn together. Whether you're married now, divorced, or separated, you can use your wedding date to determine your marriage karma as well as the spiritual purpose for the union. If not legally married, use the date on which you first consummated the relationship or became intimate.

Remember, your partner has the same number as you. So, it could be your lesson or your partner's. One of you is the student, and the other is the teacher. Roles can be reversed from time to time, too. If a relationship has failed or ended badly, it's obvious someone has chosen not to complete their study. If you're the teacher, you may be at your wits' end knowing you can't give a bad "student" a good grade. This information may help you.

If you're the student, still trying to ace a test, the following is a cheat sheet to use. Some of you may have reached a point in the commitment where you feel safe and secure. Perhaps you and your partner have already graduated to a higher level in the relationship. If not, read on for more insight.

Your Love Lesson Number

Here's the formula to uncover your marriage karma and Love Lesson number.

Add together the month, day, and year of your wedding, and reduce that number to a single digit. Here's an example:

$$\text{June 1, 1960} = 6 + 1 + 1 + 9 + 6 + 0 = 23 = 2 + 3 = 5$$
The Love Lesson number is 5.

The Nine Love Lessons

Love Lesson #1

At some point in a number-one union, one partner must learn to let go of the ego and create a selfless love. Usually, one person is guilty of being self-centered. Sometimes the world revolves around one spouse rather than the couple itself. It may be that the wife stays home while the husband is the sole breadwinner. Therefore everything is centered on the moneymaker's success and agenda. This is fine if both parties agree to such an arrangement, but what if you have two competitive people? Each wants to be number one! There is a tendency for silly, little problems to escalate into major disagreements. People who marry young, in their teenage years or early twenties, are often found to be in a number-one marriage. The individuals may also be fiercely independent types who are used to getting their way or perhaps were born an only child. This marriage may require some patience, but once the lesson of "team-work" is accomplished and ego issues are worked out, the couple can be a dynamite duo. Just replace the "me" with "we."

Love Lesson #2

It's important that both parties feel they are working together and sharing the same goals and ideals. Your lesson is to be supportive of your spouse and help make their dreams come true as well as your own. The downside to a number-two commitment is that one party may feel as if they are always sacrificing their own goals to promote the partner's. This could eventually lead to resentment. Honoring one another's ambitions is very important. In this type of marriage, the duo is learning the mechanics of a relationship— what it takes to make it work, and balancing individual needs with those of the couple. In some number-two marriages, one partner is much more committed or "in love" than the other. To keep the union stable and strong, it is important that both contribute equally to the marriage. For example, if the husband spends all free time with his buddies while the wife turns down invitations with friends and waits for him, there will be disaster down the road. Treat your spouse like you want to be treated.

Love Lesson #3

The basis for this union is to learn to communicate effectively. But it's also important to be a good listener. If your wedding day reduces to a three, you and your mate should learn to loosen up and have fun, take more chances in life, and be creative. Friendships and travel could play an important role in the marriage. You want to make sure the in-laws don't invade your space. Try to keep extended family out of your business, or there will be trouble. Once you have learned the lessons the number three wishes to teach, you'll feel your spouse is your best friend. You can talk to them about anything. This couple will have plenty of mutual friends and enjoy similar interests and hobbies. However, the most important lesson is worth mentioning again—communication is the key. Usually, one of you will have a problem expressing deep feelings. Either you didn't feel safe to show emotions as a child or you don't know how to do so effectively. The other partner is usually a talker. So by the two of you coming together, you're learning how important communication really is in a marriage.

Love Lesson #4

The lesson here is about stability versus passion. The partners in this union are meant to build a family and solid home base. There is a need for stability and structure. This is the traditional marriage. The couples wed on this day are more likely than the other numbers to go to counseling to work out problems. The challenge is to prevent the marriage from growing stagnant and stale; to keep things fresh and exciting. Home and family are the main reasons for "getting together," but don't forget about passion. Many times these couples settle down and get stuck in a daily grind. They forget about having fun together, and the thought of romance is a distant memory. At some point in the marriage, one partner will say, "I still love him/her. But I'm not 'in love.'" How sad! But it doesn't have to be that way. For example, a woman becomes a mother and finds it hard to be a firecracker in the bedroom. She's exhausted and tired from chasing kids around all day. One day she sends the little ones to stay with grandma and plans a seductive weekend for her hubby. She has found a balance between the daily monotonous routine and spontaneity.

Love Lesson #5

Your lesson is to be open to change. You absolutely must be ready and willing to accept transition. One spouse may be childish, or fancies the notion of being footloose and free. This person probably wasn't really ready to settle down but felt pressure to do so, either by family or society. To keep both people happy, this marriage needs to sustain a certain amount of excitement, change, and fun. Sometimes the number five indicates infidelity, but not always. One way to reduce the likelihood of cheating is for both partners to be sexually spontaneous with one another. A healthy sex life is very important in keeping this relationship on the right track. Many challenging circumstances arise to teach the couple about being adaptable. For example, you may have to move clear across the country because of a job promotion, in-laws may move in, or one partner's needs may change drastically as the years progress. This relationship is tested most during the midlife crisis. On the positive side, it could be the most fun-filled marriage of all the numbers. The couple that plays together stays together.

Love Lesson #6

Structure and discipline are key words for the six relationship. This marriage tends to be traditional. One of the partners wants the white picket fence, dinner on the table at five, and 2.5 kids. This works great if the other person desires the same. If not, the relationship could get boring and grow stagnant. However, if the couple recognizes how important it is to be open to change without damaging the original foundation, the marriage thrives and prospers. Usually one person is strict, bossy, or a "dictator." The other is submissive until they can no longer tolerate not being considered an "equal." When this happens, the dictator must bend to keep the marriage alive, or it will end. The lesson is to learn to make decisions together, be open to change, and honor one another. If learned, this could be one of the strongest ties, a bond never to be broken. The number-six marriage can weather any storm. This couple is voted "most likely to celebrate their fiftieth wedding anniversary."

Love Lesson #7

"Have I met my soul mate? Am I paying back karma from another lifetime? What can I learn from this crisis we're going through? Why are we really together?" These are some of the questions that a person in a number-seven marriage may ask. This commitment is supposed to be a spiritual one. The two are brought together to grow and tap in to the "higher" self as they explore the real meaning of life and love. These marriages are likely to be spiritually blessed or include a religious ceremony. Because this relationship is built on spiritual principles, the couple's belief in God will be tested. There may be challenges and crises, but they will overcome them, and the union will grow stronger. These are the couples who know they can make it through anything. The downside is that one person may be spiritually evolved and growing while the other has no faith and is at a standstill in life. There could be trust and jealousy issues, or one partner may sabotage the other's efforts. But if the relationship is special, both will look at the marriage as a spiritual gift, and continue to explore its depths.

Love Lesson #8

This can be a very materialistic marriage. One or both partners are looking for security. A person with a number-eight wedding day could marry for money. On the negative side, money may be used as a control weapon. Perhaps there's a workaholic or a shopaholic in this relationship. Finances will be an issue and a cause for argument during hard times. One of two scenarios plays out: the couple must learn hard lessons about money and struggle financially, or they are so money-driven that they work all the time. Thus, there's no chance to really enjoy the relationship. If money is their god, the marriage is headed for trouble. If they look less at the material side and focus more on the spiritual wealth of the union, they will be prosperous in all ways. The lesson here is to understand what's really important; that all of the money in the world can't replace true love. I have seen couples who grew to understand this lesson start out with meager possessions and rise to great financial status.

Love Lesson #9

Completing karma is what the number-nine marriage is all about. This couple will learn many lessons about "breaking down and rebuilding." There is not just one single issue here. Often there are many, and they could include all of the lessons from the previous numbers. What's the most special gift associated with this number? If the couple breaks up, divorces, or separates, they have a chance to try again to "get it right." They feel such a strong connection to the other that they *must* make the relationship work. The marriage can be rebuilt on a stronger foundation. These are the souls that have made a contract or a promise in previous lifetimes to right any wrongs. They have much karma to work out. If the marriage is happy, they should understand that their karma is probably finished, and now it is time to reap the rewards of a blessed and happy union.

Spiritual Love

As you've read in previous chapters, one of the main reasons a soul comes back to be with another soul is love. Whether it be to work something out in a karmic marriage or with an intense lover, I have found that many souls indeed reincarnate time and time again together. That's why you'll sometimes hear someone say, "We've been together in many lifetimes!" when they speak of their mate and sometimes even their ex! If you're one who speaks of the latter, you're probably still searching for a deeper type of love. You know on some level it exists, but how and where do you find it? I know this sounds like an old cliché, but love comes from within first . . . inside yourself. Hear me out.

Love is like air. I think we need it to survive. Without love, our lives are empty, lonely, and incomplete. It really doesn't matter what kind of love it is, as long as we can feel it and allow our hearts to breathe it in. It can be as simple as the love between two friends or as strong as the unconditional love of a mother for her child.

When we were children, we fantasized about who we'd fall in love with. The happily-ever-after fairy tales provided us with a picture of what love was supposed to be like. Little girls dream of marrying their handsome prince. Little boys long to be the knight in shining armor slaying the dragons for their princess. The older we get, the more we realize fairy tales aren't real. Love like that doesn't exist. Or does it? Deep down, we still have hope, and we search endlessly until we find that special someone.

Being in love can bring many emotions, including joy, compassion, kindness, and even fear. Yes, fear, because once we have found something so wonderful, we fear we will lose it. This is where jealousy, control, and manipulation can rear their ugly heads in a loving relationship.

To better understand how to deal with these overpowering emotions, we need to work on our spiritual side. Spiritually healthy individuals will find no reason to fear. They trust that the love they give will be received and returned. In today's society, every couple shares baggage from previous relationships. Some share heavy karma.

I tell my clients that there's something to learn from every relationship. No relationship is a waste of time. The most frustrating relationships are the ones that offer the most growth. We learn from experience. People learn more from crisis and pain than from joy and success. I am not suggesting that anyone stay in a bad or abusive relationship. But if we do find ourselves in a negative relationship, we should look at it as a learning experience, and move on. We should grow from it.

Contrary to popular belief, we do not draw lovers for our personal growth. We draw them for our soul's growth. Our ego tells us we feel good when we are with that special someone. We think marriage will help us keep that special feeling. Love has nothing to do with our personalities or our egos. Our ego or personality is what first attracts us to one another. But on a deeper level, it's our soul that knows what we need. It makes the connection with that which we call true love.

Have you ever heard the expression "He captured my soul"? Actually, it's more like a magnetic pull! Our soul connects with another's for the sake of learning, growing, and loving. Therefore it is important that both partners work to build the spiritual side of their relationship. They do that by placing their egos aside and making compassion, kindness, and unconditional love a priority. A spiritual relationship has no room for jealousy or betrayal. I tell my clients, "You are a reflection of your partner's soul. We are mirrors of one another. What you lack or what your soul needs, it will draw to you, to fill itself. Your partner's soul needs what you have." That's why opposites attract. When we fail to allow our higher selves to shine through in a relationship, we end up despising the very things that drew us to one another in the first place.

For example, my client Lori was very attracted to Paul because he seemed so self-assured and in control. He was always cool and collected. Paul was drawn to Lori for her sensitive emotional side. She could express her feelings freely. As the relationship progressed, Lori grew tired of Paul's "cocky" attitude. He never seemed to show any emotions toward her. She hated that he could be so distant. Paul was starting to tire of Lori's emotional mood swings. He became easily irritated when she wanted to talk about their relationship. When scenarios like this take over, know that we are shutting out our higher selves. Our personalities are taking over and our egos are kicking in.

If we veer too far off our spiritual path, the relationship will end. Most of the time we need to forgo the ego's needs first in order to achieve what is best for our heart and soul. Oftentimes my clients will pray for and affirm a very specific type of relationship. The universe hears all requests, but seldom does it honor those requests unless they are for our highest good or will teach us a lesson so we can grow spiritually. First and foremost, I feel we get what we need for our soul's growth before anything else, and, yes, for some people that means a difficult lesson.

No relationship is ever going to be perfect. There will always be ups and downs and twists and turns to deal with. But if one person is putting their heart and soul into a relationship, and the other works only on the ego level, the relationship will be very difficult to maintain. It is then up to the enlightened partner to know when to walk away. They must accept the fact that the ego-driven lover will not permit the relationship to be a spiritual one.

For their own growth and ultimate happiness, they must either leave the relationship or accept the other person totally, without trying to change them. Sometimes by leaving, the ego-driven partner is forced to deal with their fear and pain. (Remember, we learn more through experiencing pain and sorrow than any other emotion.) In some cases, the person learns and grows from the experience, and the couple may reunite. Many times they do not, because walls have been built up over the years through past mistrusts and betrayals.

The best thing you can do to better a relationship is to work on yourself first. You have to be healthy before you can draw a healthy relationship to you. If you're not spiritually developed, you may continue to draw challenging mates with heavy issues.

Acceptance also plays a big part in the success of relationships. It is important to accept the other person, but it is equally important to accept who you are. If you like yourself, other people will like you. It's that's simple. If you accept yourself, you will draw others' acceptance. People are like magnets. We draw things, sometimes unknowingly, to ourselves. Sometimes a client will say to me, "The only kind of men I draw are jerks!" With just that one sentence, she was sabotaging her chances for meeting a good guy. She was putting that negative thought out into the universe, and will undoubtedly continue to attract undesirable partners because she affirms that thought. She accepts the idea that she isn't good enough to draw positive people to her. Everyone has a self-image of themselves, what they believe to be true. We get our self-image from our parents, our teachers, and our friends, and these days, the media also influences how we think of ourselves.

Growing up, if we were told we were smart, we did well in school. If a little girl is told she is pretty, she feels pretty and acts pretty, and therefore others see her confidence in her looks, and admire her. If children are abused or are told they are stupid, they feel insecure and unworthy of being loved. We project what we think we are. What we've been conditioned to believe about ourselves since birth is how we act. Then when we grow up, we carry this self-image to the outside world and into relationships. If our self-image is poor, we will not fare well in any type of relationship. We definitely need to work on ourselves before a healthy relationship with someone can materialize.

Knowledge is power. Understanding why you feel the way you do and the conditions in your upbringing are important in order to know what to change. Once you do, you can work on those issues, perhaps through therapy. When you no longer expect failure, you can't manifest it. Another wonderful way to create more acceptance and become more fulfilled from a soul perspective is to understand the true meaning of why you are here and know your life's purpose. Once you are fulfilled, you won't need a partner to fulfill you, and therefore will only accept, choose, and draw healthy people to you.

Your Soul's Purpose

For some people, their purpose in life is to lend support. For others, it is to teach. Some are here to heal, and others are here to share with the world their talent for music or writing. There are people who fulfill their purpose in a big way, like Princess Diana or Mother Teresa. Their efforts affected the entire world. Yet others humbly serve mankind without any appreciation or recognition at all. Many will touch just one person's life, and make a difference. Both kinds are just as important.

Learn the difference between ego and soul. Decide if you are doing something in your life out of a need to get recognition, appreciation, or attention, or if you are working off an unselfish desire to help people. The basic reason we are all here on this earth plane is to be of service to others. We are not here to see how much money we can make or how famous we can become. That is an ego-driven existence.

The basis for our being is love. The more of that we put out into the universe, the more we get back. If we are on the right path, things come very easily. If we encounter obstacle after obstacle and things never go right in our lives, this is a good indicator that we are not on the right road, and it is time to examine what we really should be doing.

If more people realized this, we would have better relationships, better-functioning families, and more peace in the world. If everyone followed this direction, prejudice and hatred would be a thing of the past. One person alone may not be able to change the entire world, but if you can change yourself, you will change your relationships for the better.

My own personal story is a case in point. For fifteen years I worked in the entertainment field. I was looking to fill a void in my heart. I was given up for adoption when I was six months old, and thus had a subconscious need for approval and love. Even though I enjoyed a loving childhood, the pain of being given away made me feel unworthy and not good enough.

Not realizing my true motives, at an early age I decided to be famous. I loved to write and told everyone I was going to a great journalist one day. I did pretty well. From age sixteen to age thirty, I worked in newspaper, radio, and television. I hosted my own television talk show, did morning-drive radio, and was the editor of a national magazine. I still did not feel fulfilled or successful, but my friends were envious. They thought I had the most glamorous life, meeting celebrities, going to the best parties, and being on television. But I never truly felt fulfilled. It wasn't easy to maintain the pace, and the excitement of my career wore thin. I had to work so hard just to maintain the level I was at that it didn't seem worth it. I worked long hours and didn't feel the rewards.

The entertainment business is cutthroat. You are at the mercy of the executive producer, the news director, or the magazine publisher. I remember back in 1985, I moved away, left my family and friends, and took a huge pay cut to accept a position at a major magazine. The job title was most impressive. Celebrities were clamoring to get a mention in my magazine. After making my way to the top, the everyday stress was unbearable, and the publisher came in nine months later and fired the entire staff. Sometimes I loved the media business, and other times I hated it. I was desperately trying to find security in a career world that offered none.

The turning point for me came one day when my husband uprooted the family to further his career. I was forced to quit my job and find new employment. When I couldn't find work in my field, I grew depressed. My ego was hurt, and I felt nothing but rejection. I knew I was good. My talents and gifts were stronger than many others who were in the positions I sought. But no matter how much effort I put out, nothing came back.

I am a very determined person, but the universe knew what was best for me. I was forced into a brand-new direction. I began studying metaphysical topics. They fascinated me, and I was soon learning everything about the science of astrology that I could. Teachers appeared in my life, offering help and guidance. It is said that when the student is ready, the teacher appears. I was ready. I started a small astrological counseling service, and hundreds of people were drawn to me, many by word of mouth. My income was climbing. Within a year, I was in an entirely new business, and a whole new world had opened up for me.

My financial picture grew bigger and brighter than I could ever have imagined. I put in long hours, but it didn't seem like work. I was helping dozens of people every week understand their spiritual path, helping them find the answers within them to solve problems and give them hope for the future. I was sharing my love and compassion with complete strangers, and people were loving me back. I grew so much emotionally. Rude remarks didn't hurt my feelings like they used to. If something negative happened, I looked for the positive in it.

Yet, back then and to this day, I do not feel that what I do is a job. It is not even a career. It is a life path. I feel as if I am helping friends in need. I share my knowledge, visions, and ideas. I feel this is part of who I am. I have found my spiritual path. Things come easily in my life. I have no desire to cover the latest breaking story on network news anymore.

I never worry about where I'll be in five years, and my relationships are better. I do not feel ego-driven. I get fulfillment when clients call and tell me I have made a difference in their lives or I've helped them through a difficult time. It doesn't matter if one person knows my name or a thousand. But I will tell you that I met more wonderful people in the first two years of my spiritual work than in fifteen years of broadcasting. I know I have touched more people's lives in a meaningful way, and they in turn have touched mine. I feel alive and I feel loved.

The difference between my two walks of life is clear: The media field was ego-driven. There was always stress, fear, or insecurity. Walking my spiritual path, I feel in control and safe, and I know I don't have to worry anymore. The universe supplies my every need. In relationships, ego needs are always different from the soul's needs. The ego looks to get its own needs met over anything else. It needs superiority. The soul's need is fulfillment, which requires delays in immediate gratification. It often means helping others before helping itself.

Many people do not find that there's a balance in their relationships. One partner is usually battling their fearful ego. Once they achieve a certain status in the relationship, they strive to maintain it and fight change. People coming from this position are thinking of themselves. They feel if they give of themselves too much, they are being used or abused. They look only at how much they can benefit from the union. Without changing these patterns, the couple stops growing together, and the universe stops working for them.

If both partners have found their own path, they will grow together. To find your path, it is good to use the talents you were born with. I use my communication abilities to counsel those in need. If you write, write a book or article that will help readers in some way. If you have a skill, pass it on by teaching it to someone else.

If you have lots of love to give, become a parent. Being a good parent is one of the best ways you can fulfill part of this destiny. If you devote your life to being of service to others, for their betterment and not your own, the universe will reward you generously. All your emotional, physical, and material needs will be taken care of. There will be no reason for stress or worry. My prayer is that everyone who is reading this book will take the time to find their spiritual path, and allow it to open up for them. Not only will your own life be more fulfilling, but the relationships around you will benefit. We all need love to survive. If we truly open our hearts and souls to the possibilities, we can all live rich, long, loving lives.

Your Life's Path and Lessons

Each sign of the zodiac has special talents. If you aren't already aware of what your talents are, the following information may help you on the road to finding your own special path for service and, ultimately, spiritual growth. Each sign also has special challenges in love, which will be discussed in the next few pages.

Aries

Aries have been given strong, sharp minds. They would do well to use their gifts in the areas of teaching, counseling, supervising, and managing. The can use their fighting spirit to stand up for causes and the rights of others.

In love, Aries need to learn to work on putting their partner's needs ahead of their own. They should strive for more of a balance in a marriage or committed relationship. They need to set the ego aside and let their hearts speak.

Taurus

Taurus are blessed with artistic talent, and many have beautiful voices. They could excel in the areas of singing, acting, artistry, or dance. It is important that they share these gifts with the universe. Taurus also have been given a good business and financial sense. They could help others with investing or managing money.

Taurus need to trust that the love they give will come back to them. They need to let go of their fear of loss and be open to change. Taurus benefits by releasing the need to possess and learning that security comes from within.

Gemini

Gemini have been given the gift of gab. They are the communicators of the zodiac. It is important that they channel these gifts into the areas of teaching, writing, counseling, and perhaps working with children.

Gemini needs to experience a variety of relationships and emotions before making a commitment. They need to learn to create strong communication in love.

Cancer

Cancer is the sign of the mother. Those born under this sign have a natural desire to nurture people. They have compassion and are very psychic. They do well in parenting roles, as ministers, daycare providers, and homemakers, and helping abused children.

Cancer's challenge in love is to let go of the past and move on. They need to feel more self-assured and deserving of love. Cancer, you do not need to smother to receive the love and security you desire. Be more trusting of the universe to bring the love you need to you.

Leo

Leo was given a talent for entertaining. They have a great sense of humor and much creativity. Leos make great actors, broadcasters, and musicians. Any type of business in which they can express creativity and love works well. Many are fine leaders and entrepreneurs.

Leo's ego needs to be set aside so their generous hearts can shine. Leo, know that you can manifest whatever it is you truly wish for. Don't be afraid to wear your heart on your sleeve.

Virgo

Virgos have virtues that include dedication and unselfish service to others. They also have healing power. They make excellent nurses, doctors, massage therapists, healthcare professionals, and teachers.

Virgo's lesson in love is to be of service. Virgo, be open to giving, but equally open to receiving love. Realize that the perfection you seek comes from within yourself. You must first be satisfied with who you are and realize that you are perfect just as you are.

Libra

Libra is a creative sign. They have also been born with a sense of justice and fairness. Libras have been given the ability to see both sides of the coin. Many do well working as lawyers, judges, marriage counselors, and professional matchmakers.

In love, Libra's lesson is to create a peaceful and harmonious spirit first within themselves. They need to be open to the beauty and simple pleasures life and love have to offer.

Scorpio

Scorpios have very deep psychological understanding. They have great healing powers and the ability to look at life and death in more spiritual terms than most people. They make great doctors, researchers, detectives, astrologers, grief counselors, and hospice workers.

Scorpio needs to avoid confusing control with security in love. They need to learn to allow their emotions to come out and play, and to express those deep, intense feelings with their partner.

Sagittarius

Sagittarius are born with an understanding of higher philosophies and a yearning for religious experimentation. They are excellent public speakers. Sagittarius would do well as teachers, politicians, lawyers, negotiators, and international diplomats. With their natural athletic abilities, they make fine personal trainers and sports figures.

Sagittarius' love lesson is a spiritual one. They need to look at love for what it is—a higher, more meaningful energy. They need to be honest and truthful with their own feelings.

Capricorn

Capricorns have strong business and organizational skills. They excel in administrative and business positions, in police work, in government and corporate jobs, and as overseers.

Capricorn needs to allow their emotional side to show, to be less cautious in opening their heart, and to have more faith in what the universe can bring them.

Aquarius

Aquarius are here to make the world a better place. They have a humanitarian nature and possess a sense of fairness. They make excellent social reformers, fundraisers, politicians, scientists, environmentalists, and evangelists.

Aquarius are here to make a difference in the world in some way. They should learn to work on detachment issues in their own personal relationships. Many are scared to get too close emotionally in a one-on-one relationship.

Pisces

Pisces have the ability to dream, to be creative. They are psychic and would work well in any type of field where they are helping others. Many Pisces own hair salons or service businesses, and many are quite wealthy because of their own business endeavors.

Pisces need to trust their feelings. If they can accept themselves for who they really are, not what others want them to be, they will prosper in love. It is also important that Pisces choose emotionally healthy mates who do not capitalize on Pisces' guilt-ridden nature.

Spiritual Development Through Following Your Life's Path

Make a list of all of your talents and skills. See where they could fit into a career choice. Many people who are doing what fulfills them in their career tell me they do not feel like what they do is actually work. It is a passion. Just as many people say they really don't know how to capture that passion or what even interests them. Perhaps you could find your life path by taking different classes that sound interesting. You could also speed the discovery process along by doing affirmations and meditations. Everyone needs a little bit of time every day to just sit and think. We are all so busy that we seldom take time to listen to our inner voice.

It's a good idea to take the time to get in touch with your creative side, too. Being creative stirs the juices. It makes you feel alive. Write. Sing. Dance. Draw. Doodle. Even cooking can be creative.

Learn to meditate. It will not only help you find answers within yourself but reduce stress as well. Meditation is much easier to do than you would think. The more you do it, the more you will find it necessary and make time for it. If you are not sure how to meditate, I suggest getting a meditation tape that can help guide you through the process. You can find a wide assortment in the health/ New Age areas of a bookstore. Many times your spirit guides will give you messages about what your direction should be. Through meditation, you can create a link to your higher self, and your subconscious will speak to you. You'll be surprised at how easily the thoughts will come.

Another way to find your soul's purpose is through your astrology chart, or natal chart. Astrologers need your time of birth, the date you were born, and the city of your birth to make a chart. The chart resembles a wheel made up of twelve sections (or houses). Each section signifies a part of your life—your past, present, and future. The planets in our solar system and where they were stationed at the time of birth show the influences that were around you at that time. Current transiting planets indicate opportunities and challenges for the native. There are three placements I look for in a natal chart to determine the soul's purpose: the nodes, the twelfth house in the chart, and the house in which the sun is placed. They are easy to recognize and fairly easy to interpret.

Many times astrologers can pinpoint exactly the client's karma and soul purpose. If a person follows their chart, things flow more easily. If a person neglects to understand what their soul's purpose is and doesn't work toward fulfilling that purpose, life becomes challenging. It's as if we are constantly being tested by the universe to help us get on track to doing our soul's work.

Astrology is like a roadmap of your life. You don't have to use your special map. You can ignore it for a while, if you choose, because you drive the car. But the more you veer off your path, the more roadblocks you'll run into and the more collisions you'll have. If you follow your map to a T, life becomes a superhighway!

Most people also don't realize that we each choose our life path before we are born. With a belief system that includes reincarnation, we all have predestined lives; there's something we are here to accomplish in our current lifetime for our soul's growth.

Of the thousands of charts I have interpreted over the years, the majority of people are here to experience growth through spiritual development, career, service, or relationships. This leads me to the next chapter, which explores the question, how old a soul are you? There are many people in this world who keep coming back lifetime after lifetime to work on issues of commitment and love. Often these souls will get involved with the same people (souls) over and over again until they "get it right" and learn their lessons. It's as if they made a pact with one another before being born into the lifetime. Sometimes the soul needs to work on a situation or dilemma that doesn't involve a mate, one that perhaps involves learning to trust their inner self or developing spiritual wisdom.

How Old a Soul Are You?

How old is your soul? The age of the soul often reflects the kind of issues or challenges it has chosen to deal with in each lifetime. It is said that the younger the soul, the harder the lessons. As we pass through each lifetime, our souls grow closer to God. We are often helped or challenged by other souls along our path. In ego-based relationships, partners often feel controlled, manipulated, or taken advantage of. If one person chooses not to work on the soul level, there is a rebellious undertone in the relationship.

I believe anyone can make any relationship work, no matter how strong the incompatibilities, if both partners are working on a soul level. If they willingly accept each other's path in life, there can be harmony. Even an old soul can learn to live with a young soul. Old souls are wiser, and young souls have much to learn from them. If they can accept their differences, they can learn much from one another.

You've heard the saying "A cat has nine lives." This very old concept, handed down generation after generation, suggests that we, as humans, have nine lifetimes. My deceased aunts taught me the formula years ago. It works!

My friend and fellow astrologer Reverend Cindy Myers has done extensive research on this theory. Over the past twenty-one years she has tested this age-old theory on over ten thousand people, and the findings have been phenomenal. The ancestors may have known something after all!

I have heard some people call this theory Chinese numerology. Others have called it lifetime numerology. This can be an important tool in finding out where you're at in terms of spiritual growth, how old a soul you are, and what lessons you need to learn, with an emphasis on relationships.

If you fail to learn your lessons in your number-one lifetime, it is believed you will repeat the number-one cycle over and over until you get it right. You can't move on to the next lifetime until you've passed the previous one. Think of someone in their first lifetime as a preschooler or kindergartner. By the time a person reaches their ninth lifetime, they'll graduate college and never have to come back!

Your Lifetime Number

Let's learn the formula first.

1. Take your day of birth, and add it to your birth month.

2. Then add the last two digits of your year of birth.
   Example: April 1, 1970 = 4 + 1 + 70 = 75

3. Reduce that number to a single digit.
   75 = 7 + 5 = 12 = 1 + 2 = 3

4. The 3 signifies a third lifetime.

The Nine Lifetimes

First Lifetime

Ones are the babies, the young souls. This is their first experience on the physical plane. They make a lot of common, basic mistakes. To them, everything is new. They stick with what they know. They appear to be childlike, immature, and sometimes selfish. Some don't believe there is a God, and even more don't believe in the hereafter.

Ones have not developed specific personality traits and learn as they go. The younger the soul, the more mistakes it makes. These folks make many. They have to work hard at everything—marriage, parenting, and making the right choices. Their biggest challenge is to learn not to live in their own little world. They must learn to take the initiative. They also need to work harder at understanding the mechanics of relationships and being more open to spiritual wisdom. They must learn where they've come from and develop faith in God.

Second Lifetime

These folks are here to work on relationships but not just those of a romantic nature. They'll try everything once and are learning that they need other people to survive. They need to learn how relationships work, their significance, and the importance of having family, friends, parents, and mates.

People in their number-two lifetime have a strong faith in God because that's what they had to learn in their previous lifetime. Their real challenges are learning to compromise, to appreciate others, and to love.

Third Lifetime

These people are cautious. They like tradition, format, and structure. They usually enjoy financial fortune. These are the salt-of-the-earth type of people who grow up in a community and never leave.

Threes avoid risky ventures and don't want to try anything "New Age." They believe in God but don't have an overwhelming faith. They tend to be good husbands and wives, are very family-oriented, and are loyal mates and friends. Their challenge is to have more faith in themselves and reach beyond what is considered safe and secure.

Fourth Lifetime

People in their fourth lifetime are rather conventional towards family and mates. They are a cross between the Threes and the Fives. They were born with certain things they want to accomplish.

There is a tendency to be cautious, like the Threes, but the Fours will at least question and explore the mysteries of life. When it comes to love, they like to pick a mate, settle down, and live happily ever after.

Most Fours have predestined mates. They are the souls that agree to come back to marry a specific person from a previous lifetime. Their relationships are usually long term. They are more likely than any other lifetime number to go into therapy to work out issues. They will miss out on some opportunities life has to offer because they don't take enough chances. However, at times Fours can be very unpredictable.

Fifth Lifetime

Born with a list of things they want to do on the physical plane, Fives are excited to be here. They are big dreamers with big plans. They are born with a huge list of things they want to experience and accomplish in this lifetime before they die. They have good luck but not overwhelming wealth. Some Fives can be very creative and make money through their own inventions. They share a strong faith in the hereafter.

Fives don't have consistency in relationships. Many enjoy more than their share of love affairs. They like variety in love. Many never marry or have been known to go without a personal relationship for years. They are comfortable with the life they are pursuing but don't find it necessary to have a mate. They are here to have fun, play, and lead an exciting life.

The challenge for Fives is to avoid hurting people with their selfishness. They have to work on ego issues. They don't intend to hurt anyone, but sometimes they do.

Sixth Lifetime

Sixes are here to inherit the world, but first they have to understand the physical plane—not just the earth, but the body as well. They need to learn how the body serves us, how to take care of it and make the most of it.

Some are born with health challenges. Once they learn that the environment is very important to their health, they can overcome any ailment. If they understand the universe and how it works, they can achieve great things and possibly become very wealthy. This is a very materialistic lifetime. You have to have this lifetime once so you can learn that it's not worth having. You can repeat this lifetime several times, but when you pass on, you learn to leave material wealth here.

Sixes are very family-oriented, but have to choose between the material world and their families. Sixes endure lots of karmic retribution in relationships. If they've laid good karma, they have loving mates. If they've laid bad karma, then relationships are difficult.

Their challenge is to let go of their materialistic needs so they can establish a balance between their personal relationships and their work.

Seventh Lifetime

This is a challenging lifetime. It is a karmic lifetime. Some Sevens are born to be totally dependent on society. This is a cruel fate. In the research done by myself and Rev. Cindy Myers, we found that many people in nursing homes and institutions were in their seventh lifetime.

Sevens are dependent on others. If not, others are usually heavily dependent on them. If they have laid bad karma in the previous six lifetimes, they pay for it in the seventh. Sevens are more likely than any other lifetime number to contemplate suicide.

The challenge is to "stick it out" in the lifetime, to the very end, and to pay all karmic debts graciously.

Eighth Lifetime

Eight is a good money lifetime. The idea is to create a better and more comfortable lifestyle for yourself, a better reality. Eights can make great changes in the world to alter the state of reality. Here you find your gurus and spiritual leaders. Financially blessed, many Eights are detached when it comes to personal relationships. They want to help the entire world, to promote love and peace and make major changes on the earth plane. They go forth to spread the word of God and usually have the money behind them to afford such a lifestyle. Their challenge is to use that spiritual nature for the highest good and stay away from manipulation.

Ninth Lifetime

Nines are happy, but outsiders tend to look at Nines as having very sad lives. Nines are closely regulated by God. If you're in your number-nine lifetime, you have no malice, wish no one harm, and can't do anything terribly wrong.

If Nines do anything deceitful, they'll get busted every time. God keeps these folks in line. If they lie, they'll get caught. If they steal, they'll go to jail. Since this is the last lifetime, they need to be ready to leave the earth without great sin. They never own a lot, don't seem to amount to much, and are not lucky financially. God makes it this way so that it's easier for them to leave the physical plane. There is less to let go of. Nines also have physical ailments. They are often uncomfortable in the body, and they seem to carry extra burdens. This also helps them let go in this lifetime and not look back.

Nines appear to have bad relationships because they attract the younger souls whom they are here to teach. Their challenge is to stay spiritual and not lose faith, no matter how hard things seem.

Okay, we've covered a lot. But the one thing that may still leave a few of you puzzled is, how do you know if the guy or girl of your dreams is your soul mate? Read on!

How to Recognize a Soul-Mate Connection

The Soul Mate Test

Take this test to determine if you are with your soul mate or if you need to continue your search!

Keep track of how many yes answers you have.

1. Do you feel happy and content just being around this person?

2. Do you feel a sense of peace and fulfillment?

3. Do you feel as if you've known this person all your life?

4. Do you feel secure in this relationship?

5. Is knowing that this person is a part of your life enough for you? (In other words, you don't need to be with them constantly.) Is it enough for you to know that this person is a part of your life until you get together again?

6. Do you instinctively know how this person feels without having to be told?

7. Is there unconditional love? Do you accept this person for who they are and not want to change anything about them?

8. Do you feel a spiritual bond and a deeper purpose as to why you are together?

9. Is the sex great, but you don't *have* to sleep together? Is just being in this person's company fulfilling enough?

10. When you look deep into this person's eyes, is there an intense, soul-stirring connection?

11. Do you live "in the moment" when you're together? (You're not thinking of what happened two days ago or what time you must get up in the morning—there's no other place you'd rather be than in the "right now"?)

12. Do you finish one another's sentences?

13. Do you feel this particular person is the love of your life?

14. Do you feel "complete" when you're together?

15. Was there a major void in your life that is now filled?

16. Was there an immediate attraction to one another?

17. Do you feel as if you've been together in a past life?

18. Has a past-life connection been shown to be possible in an analysis of your astrological chart?

19. Have you done past-life regression work that confirms this person is a soul mate?

Count your yes answers, and look below:

13–19: Yes—definitely a soul mate!

8–12: Very likely a soul mate, but need more past-life regression work to confirm.

4–7: More likely a past-life connection rather than a soul mate.

1–3: Sorry, keep searching. Perhaps this is only a karmic tie.

Here are some good indicators that the relationship you're in is not a soul-mate connection:

1. You don't want to be apart for a single second.

2. You think of this person every waking moment and are anxious until you see them again.

3. You're worried they will dump you one day.

4. You're jealous of this person's friends, family, and exes.

5. You get butterflies in your stomach just thinking about this person.

6. You anxiously wait for their calls.

7. You can't wait to have sex!

8. You're so wrapped up in this person that other parts of your life suffer. You take time off from work, play hooky, and stop spending as much time with your friends.

9. You worry if the relationship is going to last.

10. You push for a deeper commitment.

11. You feel a need to rush into the relationship and fall head over heels in love.

12. If you have to ask, this person is probably not a soul mate.

13. You feel you need to lie or manipulate to get your way.

Making and Breaking a Soul-Mate Connection

You may meet your soul mate in the most unusual places or under the strangest circumstances. Fate is what initially brings you together. It's all about destiny and timing. You may meet your soul mate at any age. Some people are only eight years old, while others don't reunite until they experience life's ups and downs and some sort of a loss so they can appreciate what they have.

Soul mates don't always stay together forever, either. You may be destined to stay together for a shorter period of time than you would prefer, usually to help one another, learn a lesson, open your heart, or repay a debt. Many people do marry their soul mate, and remain happily married forever and ever, amen. Some soul mates create negative karma and end up breaking up because of ego-based issues or bad judgment. If you are one of those people who has lost your soul mate, and there is no chance of getting back together, know that you will likely meet again in another lifetime if there is still unfinished business. But don't deny yourself a relationship with a new mate with whom you can create new, loving karma.

All of our relationships are created to fulfill a purpose. We are a reflection of our partner's soul. Many times our partner can provide whatever we need for our soul's growth. Even so-called bad relationships are precious because we can learn from them. As stated earlier, we grow more from sorrow and pain than from joy and happiness. A strong bond develops between people when they experience a hardship together. So look at trouble spots in your relationships as opportunities to grow and learn. They can be very positive influences.

Actually, it's a good idea to remove the words "trouble" and "problems" from your vocabulary. If you think your lover is a problem, it's possible he is apt to be one of your many teachers in life. What can you learn from him and his actions? Replace the word problems with opportunity. Then you'll have fewer problems in your relationships. Many people say, "Someday our relationship will be good. Someday I'll be happy." If you are capable of being happy someday, you are capable of being happy right now. It's all in the way you look at things.

Basically we enter relationships with the idea that our partner can fill our life with love and happiness. We expect unconditional love and approval from our mate. That's what we get in the beginning of a relationship or marriage, but as time drags on and years go by, that's not always the case. Our need for romance and fulfillment becomes a tall order because our lover is expecting to gain the same things from us. Therefore, expectations are not met, and both partners start pointing fingers and blaming one another for not meeting their needs. As time goes on, the relationship suffers.

Counseling soul mates, heartbroken lovers, and dumped loners, I've learned a thing or two about making relationships work. Because the majority of soul-mate connections are related to karma, these unions can be the most tested. Here are a few tips from lucky lovers I've counseled to help you make a relationship work.

How to Avoid a Breakup with Your Soul Mate

One the biggest mistakes people make in relationships is that they move too fast. I know clients who on the first date are thinking about walking down the aisle. They wonder, is this the one? They go from point A to point M in a matter of hours and are extremely disappointed if a second date doesn't occur. Have you heard the phrase "too hot not to cool down"? Well, some relationships start off with a bang and fizzle out rather quickly because the two can't maintain the intensity over a long period of time. Take a new relationship one step at a time and one day at a time. Build it on a solid foundation so if there is a crisis (and there will be), the relationship won't crumble or, worse yet, come crashing down.

Another mistake people make in a new love affair is that they want to spend every single moment with their new amour. Even if both parties feel the same way, you'll eventually get tired of one another 24/7, so don't give up your friends and other interests. Those individual interests make you more enticing and give you something to talk about and share. Also, don't call your lover ten times a day because then there's no chase. Remember, if someone has to chase you, they feel as if they've invested more in the relationship, which leads me to my next suggestion . . .

Don't give 110 percent!!!! What? Yup. Don't go overboard. Most women and a few men I know tend to go overboard when they first get into a relationship. They set bad patterns in which they do all the giving and their partner doesn't have a chance to reciprocate. For example, Joan meets Greg. After the first date, she asks him over for dinner. Then she calls him every morning before work and every evening. She volunteers to do his laundry and cook for him during the week. She asks him to go on a vacation, and foots the entire bill. Joan is doing everything! She loves to do these things. It makes her happy, and she's thrilled to have someone in her life whom she's so infatuated with. She's in love! But a few months down the road, after the love dust settles, Joan is complaining that Greg never takes her anywhere and doesn't do anything for her. Joan feels she is doing everything! And she is. But she set these patterns, and patterns are hard to break.

So my advice is not to give too much. Make it equal. If Greg pays for dinner, then Joan cooks the next night. She then waits for him to ask her out again. She takes the relationship day by day. She calls, and then waits for him to call. Is that playing a game? No, it's creating balance and equality in a relationship. It's giving the other person an opportunity to invest their time and energy in the relationship rather than one person taking the entire lead. And anything in which we invest our time, energy, and money is valuable to us, or we wouldn't make such an effort, now would we? Build the relationship together with each person putting into it. Don't try to build or push it yourself. I guarantee that relationships like Joan and Greg's don't last long when one partner does all of the giving. That person ends up feeling like a victim. Old habits are hard to break, so don't create any at the onset of a new love affair. What happens in the first few weeks of a new romance sets the stage and pattern for a long time to come.

Another suggestion I have is don't push the fast-forward button after a few dates. Your partner may be taking their time in getting to know you and wants to see how things progress. If you move too quickly and announce, "I feel you're the one I've been looking for all my life. I see marriage in our future," you could intimidate the gal or guy of your dreams. Keep your thoughts and ideas to yourself for the first three months unless your partner is on the same wavelength as you. Otherwise, you'll find the object of your affection running scared.

Probably the best advice I can give you in regard to relationships is that every relationship goes through a testing period. It's inevitable. A relationship will be challenged to see what it's made of. Most commonly, one person will start to withdraw a little from the relationship at some point, and the other person panics. Oh, now they're losing interest! They don't love me anymore. There must be someone else! Then the insecurities come out and arguments start, most often over something really silly. The couple breaks up. One may date someone else, while the other is left home alone waiting for a call to get back together. What do you do?

First, this period is a time for both individuals to reassess the relationship itself and decide just how important it is to them. I have seen time make hearts grow fonder. Sometimes months and, yes, even years heal. It can happen. If you are the jilted party, do not cry, kick, beg, moan, and suggest a long, drawn-out heart-to-heart talk. Don't try to fix things. Give your lover space and act with the utmost integrity and class. Don't get jealous or try to make them jealous. Be honest and forthright and give them time. Do not call or send cards, but let them know the door is open if you haven't moved on by the time they decide what they want to do.

It seems that every relationship that has been ongoing for at least a year or more and is heading for the altar will be tested like this. If you are the "dumped" individual, the probability of getting back together is good if you handle yourself well in this type of crisis. Remain cool, calm, and collected, and get on with your life. Often the two of you will get back together. If not, you can plead until the cows come home, but your partner won't want you back anyway. At least you have your self-respect and aren't laying any negative karma.

If you've taken the test, and decide it's time to continue your search for someone new, read on!

Using Meditation to Find Your Soul Mate

If you can already know how to meditate, great! If not, you should learn to do so. It can be very helpful in unlocking subconscious thoughts about the past, present, and future. If you want to know if you've already met your soul mate, meditation is a great tool for confirmation. If you know you haven't and want to gain a clearer picture of who's out there for you, meditation can help. If you find that the CDs and recorded do-it-yourself meditations don't work for you, you may want to locate a past-life regression therapist, especially one that deals with soul mates.

When I released my first meditation CD, it was titled *Discovering Your Soul Mate* and sold out in the first year. There were so many people anxiously seeking answers. Before I released the CD to the public, I tried it out on a few guinea pigs. My one friend, who is a Cancer, has always dated men named Jack. It seems Jacks are always drawn to her. In fact, she's married to one today. She's dated Andrews and Scotts, too, but the ex-Jacks were the most difficult relationships to let go of. They cheated, lied, and hurt her very badly, but for some reason she would never leave. Even after they had broken a relationship off with her, this Cancer gal would hang on. Crying and praying for their return was her daily routine.

She admitted that she had only agreed to do this soul-mate meditation to patronize me. In fact, she had never tried to meditate before and felt she wouldn't see anything anyway. After the meditation, she opened her eyes, and tears were streaming down her face. They were tears of joy! I asked her what was wrong. She replied, "Nothing. I have never felt this much love in my entire life."

What had she seen? She had seen herself on a military fort dressed in a prairie gown. She guessed the period to be around the late 1800s. A man dressed in a soldier's uniform turned to her and hugged her. She actually felt his warm embrace in the meditation. He looked her deeply in the eyes and said, "I love you. I will never leave you!" Then he left.

My friend said she then got a bad feeling in her stomach, and opened her eyes. More than likely this soldier husband went off to war and never fulfilled his promise to her. He was killed and never returned to his beloved. But there's more. On his lapel, he wore a name tag that read "Jack Robbins"! In this current lifetime, my friend is still searching for her "Jack." Desperate to find him and reconnect with that special love from a century ago, she draws other Jacks to her instead. She concluded that she will not leave her current husband to find this one true love and soul mate, but at least she now understands why she draws men named Jack and refuses to let go, even in the worst of circumstances.

Then we have another friend of mine, named Sharlotte, who also did the meditation. She, however, was not pleased with the result. In fact, she was very angry with me. "I never want to do this again!" she shouted. "I don't like what I saw." I asked her to share what she had seen. When she went back to a prior lifetime, Sharlotte saw herself surrounded by people she loves in this one. But she had a crying, wailing baby in her arms that she wanted nothing to do with. She understood that this child was hers but felt such a strong responsibility and a tremendous burden because of this infant. She looked down into the face of her baby and gasped. The baby was her current husband in this lifetime!

He had come back to take care of her in present time. She said she always feels such a strong protective feeling toward him and admits he is a big baby! Sometimes she feels he is a burden, but she truly loves him. These two people reincarnated to come back together. They fell in love rather quickly, and both believed they were soul mates after only a few dates, destined to be together!

I have been on a national lecture tour this past year. I speak in major cities all over the United States. Thousands of people have come to my lectures and have shared with me what they have learned during our group soul-mate meditations. A number of people have meditated only to find they don't recognize the person they see. In these cases, the participants are getting a glimpse of their future soul mates. They will likely meet up with them at a predestined time, when the time is right and they are ready.

My friend Paula sat through one of my meditation sessions in Chicago, and saw a dark-haired man. She, too, didn't recognize him but described him in great detail. As we boarded the plane to return home, she gasped. "That's the same guy I saw in my meditation. He looks exactly the same!" I told her to go sit by him and start up a conversation. She chickened out. Did she lose her big chance to meet her soul mate? Will she have another opportunity? Only time will tell.

Another friend, named Cindy, who meditates all the time, saw herself sitting on a park bench when she tried the meditation. Her soul mate was not a distinct person but rather a strong male energy. He spoke to her telepathically and told her he would not be with her physically in her current lifetime but he would be with her spiritually. He assured Cindy he was always there for her, like a guardian angel to help her, but she would physically have to walk this current life path alone. She, too, had tears in her eyes but felt comforted by his presence.

Other people who have been in my workshops report that they don't see a specific person, but colors. The deeper the color and the closer it appears to you, the sooner a soul mate will come into your life. If the color appears faint and far away, your soul mate may still be at a distance in time. If you see a pink light, that signifies a lover. A green hue means someone is coming to help you heal. Purple is a spiritual color, and you can learn much from this new acquaintance.

Because meditation unlocks subconscious memories, it can help you discover the memories your soul still retains. All of the answers are within you. You must just be willing to trust your inner voice and intuition. Meditation is one of the best tools I have found to help connect you to other lifetimes and those people whom you have loved. Then when you meet again in a current incarnation and feel something a little extra special between you, it helps confirm those feelings.

What if you already know you're *not* with your soul mate, but instead are stuck in a dead-end relationship you refuse to leave? This next chapter will help you determine whether the guy or gal you're with is indeed a soul mate or if you're merely doin' time with a cell mate!

Still Stuck in Love Prison?

Cell Mates—Learning to Unlock the Ties That Bind

Do you feel trapped in your relationship? Are the walls closing in? Are you a prisoner of love?

If you're in a relationship that can't be saved and you want out, you owe it to yourself to decide what is keeping you there. If you haven't found your soul mate yet, what's keeping you from experiencing true happiness? If you feel imprisoned and in a dead-end commitment, you owe it to yourself and your partner to get out. Why procrastinate? There are lots of excuses. I think I've heard them all, but I've narrowed them down to the top five for this chapter. If you see your excuse listed, you're not alone. Millions of people are unfulfilled but "hanging in there" for one reason or another. Read on if you're living with your cell mate!

Maria's Top Five Excuses
People Stay in Bad Relationships

1. Fear of being alone.

2. Money.

3. A lack of self-esteem and confidence.

4. Procrastination ("I'll leave one day!" I promise).

5. Guilt—the relationship is not bad enough to leave but not good enough to stay in.

The Cell Mate Test

If you're not sure if the guy or gal you're with is truly a "cell mate," ask yourself the following questions.

1. Are you depressed when you're together?

2. Do you feel trapped in this relationship?

3. Do you argue more than you talk?

4. Can you recall the last time you said "I love you"?

5. Do you avoid sex as much as possible?

6. Are you attracted to other people?

7. Do you resent the guy or gal you're with?

8. Do you make plans for the future that include your mate?

9. Are you excited about your future together?

10. Can you imagine spending the rest of your life together?

11. Do you honestly think you'll stay together forever?

Now add up all of your no answers, and follow the guide below.

8–11 no answers: Definitely a cell mate. Get out as soon as you can afford to! You feel like a prisoner, and the relationship will eventually end at some point.

5–7 no answers: You can love them or leave them. It's not that bad but can be fixed. However, it may be a good idea to take a breather and see what it feels like being single for a while. If you truly enjoy the break, make it permanent. If not, you can likely crawl back home.

1–4 no answers: You can work things out. It may take some time, but you have options. I suggest a few therapy sessions to see what the problems are. Sometimes you just need to reinvent the relationship or create change so it doesn't get stale.

Let's take a closer look at the top five reasons people stay in a bad relationship.

Reason Number 1: Fear of Being Alone

Are you happier and less stressed when your mate is out of town on a business trip or on a weekend hunting trip? Do you welcome their absence? Do you get depressed or feel anxiety when they return? Are you pushing them out the door? Here's an example. Mr. Wonderful leaves for a few days to visit the relatives. You're asked to join him on the trip but decline because you'd rather have some free time. As soon as he pulls out of the driveway, you feel ecstatic! You're making plans to do lots of things and looking forward to filling your hours with fun. Maybe you'll visit friends, go shopping, clean the house, or read a novel. Close to the time of his impending return, you feel doomed, as if you're trapped again. Oh, no! There are only a few precious hours left until he comes home! You wish you had more time. Does this sound familiar?

Maria's answer: You're not afraid of being alone, you're just afraid of being alone *forever.* Who says you will be? Look back at all the people you dated in the past and all the opportunities you had for romance that you passed up. Yes, it may take some time to meet someone you really like. If you truly want a relationship, there will be one out there for you. But you need to get out of the house—it's not the pizza delivery guy!

Reason Number 2: Money

Money is another big reason many people stay together. You can't afford to leave. Every time you plan to, something comes up that forces you to spend the money you had saved up. Maybe you've acquired lots of equity in a home or perhaps have financial obligations you need to get rid of first.

Maria's answer: Money and convenience are two big reasons that people stay in relationships long past their prime. Know that you may have to downsize and cut back on expenses, but don't you deserve more? Get an extra part-time job. Do you really need all of those new shoes? What's more important, personal inner peace and happiness or the bigger house? Need health insurance? Get a new job that will cover it. No more excuses.

I know a lady who was in a seventeen-year relationship. She was unhappy for sixteen of them, married to an abusive alcoholic who wouldn't seek help. Five years ago she began to strategize. She said nothing of her plans to leave until she was financially set. She saved all of her money and spent his to pay off their joint credit card and other bills. She had thousands of dollars saved up, enough to make a decent down payment on her own home. She went back to school, got a degree, and landed a better job. Then she left. Today she's dating someone with whom she's head over heels in love, and she has no financial concerns.

Reason Number 3: A Lack of Self-Esteem and Confidence

"I don't know how I'll make it on my own. No one will ever want me. I need someone. Anyone is better than no one." These are all excuses I hear from people who suffer from a lack of self-esteem. Perhaps their opinions were shot down by the very person they're in a relationship with. If this is the case, that's emotional abuse. Once a person recognizes that they suffer from low self-esteem, they can do something about it. It can be a rather long haul, depending on how low they feel. Sometimes depression is a cause, too. Those who stay in a relationship for these reasons find life boring and have little motivation to do anything for themselves. Some feel unworthy and unlovable.

Maria's answer: This one is plain and simple: see a therapist and work on self-worth issues. Get to the root of the problem. As a person gains understanding, they gain freedom. Do things that make you feel good about yourself for yourself. Find a job or hobby that you excel in. It will help boost your self-esteem and self-worth. Include affirmations in your morning ritual that stress what a wonderful person you are!

Reason Number 4: Procrastination

If you put off leaving when you know you should, you're putting off happiness, inner peace, and quality of life. Many of my clients tell me that one day they'll leave—after the kids are grown, when they have enough money, after they finish school, when they lose weight, etc. Their excuses are never-ending. The problem with procrastination is, the day never comes to leave. There always seems to be a reason you can't go. If you really want a piece of chocolate cake, you won't procrastinate. If you want to buy a new outfit and have the money to do so, you won't deny yourself. If you don't procrastinate on the little things in your life, why would you procrastinate on things that really matter, like being happy?

Maria's answer: Set deadlines and goals for yourself, little ones every day. Build a support system of friends and family around you to give you a kick in the butt if you need it. Women who have health problems usually see their condition lessen or clear up once they leave a negative relationship. Women usually suffer from stress, anxiety disorder, panic attacks, etc., if they have endured years of unhappiness. One woman I know had a severe case of panic attacks that started when her current boyfriend moved in. He was pressuring her to get married and was smothering her. She just couldn't say no. She kept trying to break off the relationship, and he kept pushing. She eventually ended up in the hospital with a heart attack. She was only forty-three years old! She ended the relationship a few months back, and has no health symptoms. Her panic attacks have miraculously vanished!

Reason Number 5: Guilt

The relationship is not good enough to stay in but not bad enough to leave. Ask yourself, how bad does it have to get? You don't want to be the "bad guy." You love the person, but you're not "in love."

Maria's answer: Where do you personally draw the line? Examine why you carry so much guilt, and recognize the fact that you are not hurting only yourself but also the person you're with. They deserve someone who truly loves them, and you do, too. A relationship without passion and romantic love eventually ends. If it doesn't, both individuals may feel as if they are just going through the motions of life. Slowly back away from the relationship. Make new friends and involve yourself in other activities without your partner.

How to Dump Anybody and Make Them Think It's Their Idea
(Based on Astrological Signs)

Still don't have the gumption to end a negative thing? Don't hang around creating more karma. It could very well be that you don't want to be the bad guy in the breakup. Sometimes it's easier to get dumped than to do the dumping.

Well, if you relate, here are a few tips to make life so miserable for your cell mate that they'll be out the door in no time. They'll think it was their idea all along to end the relationship. Then you're off the hook. But be forewarned: some signs of the zodiac are harder to budge than others. Some of these suggestions are downright mean and nasty. However, there are some romantic diehards that don't give up. So if you really don't care about laying bad karma or hurting someone's feelings, and just want out, read on!

How to Get Rid of an Aries

In love, Aries men and women need to know they are number one with you. They don't like to play second fiddle to anyone or anything. Move them way down your totem pole! Act disinterested in what they're doing. Criticize their abilities to succeed. This zodiac sign likes to be in charge, so don't follow a bossy Aries' rules. Do just the opposite of what they tell you. Aries is also a fire sign, so many are action-oriented beings. They lose interest in things quickly anyway and can't stand boring people.

So, be boring! Be slow. Don't jump when they tell you to. There's a surefire way to lose a Ram . . . remember, they love a good chase, so let them know you're not going anywhere and that you'll be around for the next eight years. The Aries will be out of your life looking for more excitement, greener pastures, and a partner that puts them on a pedestal.

Here's what you tell 'em: "I have nowhere else to go, so I'm guaranteeing you that I'll never leave you, even though I don't think you're all that."

How to Lose a Taurus

Since Taurus are creatures of habit, this sign will be hard to nudge out the door. In fact, you may have to give them a good swift kick to get them to do anything! Bulls hate change. They want things to stay the same. They are slow to make moves. A Taurus will think things over and over and over again before making any big decisions. Make absolutely sure you want out of this relationship, because once Taurus makes up their mind to leave, they're gone for good. It takes a lot to get a Bull to that point, but when you do, it's truly over. This sign appreciates good food and the comforts of home. They have a favorite chair in their house that no one dares sit in. They are also very money conscious. Food, money, and sex are very important to a Taurus, not necessarily in that order.

Are you sure you want to leave? Then hide the remote control, change the furniture around every other week, don't have sex, spend all of their money on frivolous things, and leave the refrigerator empty. Eventually they'll have had enough, and that famous Taurus temper will come out, throwing you completely out of their life.

What to tell a Taurus: "I just cashed in your retirement fund to buy this new mink coat and diamond ring. You'll have to cook your own dinner while I'm on my cruise to Hawaii. No, dear, not tonight. I've got a headache." Repeat this last sentence every day for at least six months.

How to Lose a Gemini

The Twins are lots of fun to be around when their good side shows through. But when the evil twin comes out to visit, a relationship can be downright nasty. They can be moody and fickle in love. You won't have to do much to send a Gemini packing. They do need someone who will communicate with them if a relationship is going to work. Being a good listener is very important, as Geminis talk all the time. Seriously, they never stop! Also, they hate it when anyone asks them where they're going and what time they'll be home. Don't expect to keep your thumb on this sign for long. Geminis also like lots of activity. They must have something going on constantly because they get bored easily. Intellectual stimulation is of utmost importance if a relationship is going to last with a Twin.

So here's what you do. Be boring. Don't talk and, most importantly, don't listen when the Gemini is talking. You must constantly keep a check on all of their activities and plan a schedule they must adhere to. Don't allow them to change their mind regarding a decision once they make a commitment (this will drive them nuts). I don't think you have to do much to get a Gemini to hit the road. All you really need to do is stop communicating with them.

What to tell them: "Shut up! I can't stand the sound of your voice. It drives me crazy!" And then say nothing else for weeks.

How to Get Rid of a Cancer

This is another sign that will be hard to kick to the curb. Cancer folks live in the past and hang on for dear life because a part of them is so insecure. They also like to mother, smother, and protect you. They have the most sensitive feelings in the zodiac. Their home and family means the world to them. They pride themselves on keeping a good home and being a good cook. Their children are their life. Cancer men and woman are usually too close to their mothers.

So here's what you do. Hurt their feelings. Tell them they're getting a little too fat for you to be attracted to them (ouch!). Criticize their mother and constantly yell at the kids. Mess up the house and remind them how much you hate living there! Don't show any emotion when the Cancer is crying. Go away for a weekend and don't call. Make them feel you don't need them. It may take a little time, but once a Cancer is emotionally wounded, they never forget!

Here's what you tell 'em: "You'd better lose some weight if you want to look sexy again. I don't ever want to see your mother again! I hate kids, dogs and cats, and your cooking!"

How to Get Rid of a Leo

In love, Leo men and women are extremely generous, but they expect to be treated like the kings and queens they perceive themselves to be. They are fussy about the way they look and their hair (the lion's mane). They like to be the boss or the head of the household. Many Leos are very social and enjoy parties and friendships. Some like to gamble. Some shop too much. Leos are very proud people. They want others to hold them in high regard. They expect their servant (i.e., you) to be loyal and trustworthy.

Here's what you do. Cheat on them! That's a surefire way to get a Leo's dander up. Show no interest in their life. Refuse to wait on them. Take over the house and announce there's a new regime. Criticize their hair and tell them they aren't as attractive as they used to be. Make fun of their friends. Cut off the credit cards. Sit home and refuse to go anywhere all weekend. Don't say thank you or appreciate anything they do. Basically, act as if they don't exist. A Leo will soon look for someone who will adore them again.

Tell them this: "You're not providing enough for me. I could do much better if I went back to my ex." Tell a Leo guy he's getting balder everyday. Mention to a Leo lady that her hair looks frumpy and that she should change her style.

How to Lose a Virgo

This sign is considered a neat-freak. Everything in their life must have order to it. Everything must be clean and tidy. They want to create a simple, comfortable world for themselves. Virgos of both sexes need to be needed. They desire to help you though any crisis and feel good when asked for advice. They analyze things way too much and worry all the time about those they love. This is one of the signs that is hard to break a relationship off with, especially the longer it goes on. They feel a duty to hang in there and take their wedding vows or commitments very seriously.

Here's what you do. Trash the house. Don't pick up after yourself. Don't take their advice when they offer it. Create lots of chaos every day. Don't allow them to help you with anything. Ignore their worries. If they're complaining or nitpicking about something, go in another room so they won't have a sounding board. Be downright rude if you need to.

Here's what you say: "I don't need you anymore. I can make it on my own."

How to Lose a Libra

Libras don't feel complete if they're not in love. They hate being alone. Being in love is very important to them, just as much as peace and harmony. They hate confrontations. They want everything to run smoothly and get upset easily if life is difficult. They despise crude behavior, vulgarity, and anything that isn't prim and proper. Many Libras are indecisive people who go back and forth and can't make up their minds. If their relationship is a happy one, any other pressures in a Libra's life can be tolerated.

Here's what you do. Create total chaos for them. Argue every time you're together. Cut off all romance and act disinterested in doing things together. Swear at them a lot. Wear smelly old T-shirts and ragged underwear to bed. Embarrass them in public. Be loud and obnoxious. Make them feel they can't depend on you. Always disagree with them and keep them confused about the stability of the relationship. Talk about your goals for the future, and make it obvious that they are not a part of them.

Tell a Libra this: Actually, don't tell them anything. Just burp, make disgusting noises, pass gas, and swear all the time. They'll get the picture, and it ain't pretty.

How to Get Rid of a Scorpio

If you choose to get out of a relationship with a Scorpio, you'd better back out of this one slowly. The rule here is you *must* make the Scorpio think it's their idea to end it. Otherwise, you're asking for it. You see, Scorpio is the strongest sign in the zodiac. Even the majority of them who are very loyal, respectable people have the ability to be vengeful if wronged. Trust me, do not use tactics like you would with any other sign to end a relationship. You could end up in traction!

I must tell you a story. I have a Scorpio client whose name is Gail. She's a wonderful, kind person. She was married for over twenty-five years to a man named Bill, and sacrificed a lot for his career. In fact, she loved him so much, she waited on him hand and foot. Gail pretty much put her own life on hold so he could succeed in his own business.

Well, finally, when the millions started rolling in, things fell apart. Gail's husband came home one day and announced he was leaving her. He said he had fallen in love with someone else who was younger, prettier, and sexier. (This man would later regret using those words!) Don't ever mess with a Scorpio woman! Gail handled it very well, it seemed. Under that cool, calm, and collected Scorpio persona was a crazed, betrayed, angry, and vengeful woman. All of you Scorpios reading this know exactly what I'm talking about.

Rather then crying and begging her husband to stay, Gail went to work plotting her revenge. First she painted yard signs that read "Susie is sleeping with a married man." Other ones written in big red letters said "slut," "whore," and few other choice words not acceptable for publication. Gail planted these all over Susie's front yard in the wee hours of the morning while everyone was sound asleep. Rush hour would begin shortly, and all of the cars driving by Susie's house would see these billboards in her front yard. Oh, I forgot to mention that another embarrassing word was left on Susie's garage door in scarlet red paint. Over the next several weeks, Gail called Susie's employers and told them about the affair she was having with her husband. She contacted the minister at Susie's church and even went so far as to communicate with members of Susie's family who assumed her "wonderful new beau" was a single, eligible bachelor.

Susie felt forced to move out of her neighborhood and eventually quit her job. After Gail was finished with Susie, she proceeded to go after the husband who by this time was shaking in his boots. The vengeful acts had caused so much stress between him and Susie that their relationship had broken off. Now Gail's husband was down on his knees, begging Gail to take him back. Most of you would think this was enough for Gail, but a true Scorpio knows "it's not over until it's over."

So Gail sweetly and deceivingly agreed to take him back under the condition that he would prove to her how much he loved her. (She had no intention of doing such a thing. She manipulated him to continue on with her revenge). Bill was more than happy to do whatever she wanted. She asked him to buy her a house in Florida. He did, and she put it in her name only. She took charge of all of the money and income, cashing in his stocks and bonds and hiding over $100,000 in cash in a linen closet. She traveled all over the country, treating her friends and family while Bill worked harder than ever to support her every whim. She copied all of the business financial records and moved every single asset into her own name in a bank in Cuba. Then, when her mission was complete, she filed for divorce. Her testimony in court about her sacrifices and Bill's adulterous affairs helped her win favor with the judge, and she was awarded the family home and part of Bill's pension plus permanent alimony. Gail moved to Florida. Bill's business went under. He filed for bankruptcy and is living in a small condo. Gail is dating but says she doesn't trust men like she used to. But her last words to me were: "Revenge is sweet. I'm not depressed. I've worked through it. Getting revenge was the best therapy!" She doesn't even think of Bill anymore. It's as if he never existed.

Now, the moral of this story is not that revenge is sweet. It's don't ever mess with a Scorpio!

What to say to a Scorpio: "Anything you want is fine with me!"

How to Lose a Sagittarius

Sag is a freedom-loving sign. These folks are positive and upbeat unless they feel trapped in a relationship or situation. Their vocabulary doesn't include the word "forever" because their philosophy is that things change. They go with the flow. They can't sit home for hours on end like a Cancer or Taurus. They enjoy traveling and going to new places. Heaven help them if they're ever without a set of wheels. In love, they need someone who gives them their freedom and doesn't badger them about where they're going and what time they'll be home. Some like to collect things like baseball cards or old coins and antiques. Many Sag men love sports, and their women often find themselves alone during football and hunting seasons. Sagittarius can also be very blunt and direct, sometimes to the point of being rude. But hey, at least they're honest.

If you want your Sagittarius to leave, here's what you do. Make demands on their time. Question their every move. Take away their car keys. Don't let them sleep late (a favorite luxury of Sag). Tell them you want them home every night by 5:00 PM and give them a rundown of what you expect them to repair around the house all weekend. Tell them you'll never ever leave them, and smother them to death. Follow them everywhere they go, even to the bathroom!

Here's what you tell a Sagittarius: "I hate my life! Nothing is ever going to be right. I want you to promise me you'll stay with me forever. Let's get married right away."

How to Get Rid of a Capricorn

Most Cappys are traditional, hardworking, and strong-willed. They have a lot of determination and strong opinions, too. They like life organized. Some of them tend to be thrifty, bordering on the cheap side. The Goat is very logical. There's not much room for emotional people or crybabies in their world. They are content with a routine and a structured environment. The family structure is important and sacred to them. They believe in honesty, loyalty, and a strong work ethic.

If you want out, flirt outrageously with your Capricorn's friends. Badger the Goat to talk about their "feelings." Cry and whine over every little thing. Spend money like crazy on useless, frivolous things. Refuse to balance the checkbook, and bounce a few checks while you're at it. Announce that you are quitting your job and need $2,000 to go on a cruise (without them). Be late when they need you to be on time. Let clutter pile up. When you're laundering their white underwear, throw a bright pink towel in the load. Let yourself go. Forget to put on deodorant, brush your teeth, or shower. That should be enough to drive your Capricorn away!

Here's what to say: "My credit cards are over the limit. Can I use yours? We need to change your work schedule so it's more accommodating for my plans. I really want to know how you feel. Please talk to me about how you feel about me. Oh, I forgot to pick up your dry cleaning and pay your cell phone bill. Dinner will be two hours late. You are so cheap I can't stand it!"

How to Get Rid of an Aquarius

There are two types of Aquarius: the introvert and the extrovert. If yours is outgoing and social, their friends, clubs, organizations, and social groups could be the center of their life. If they're the loner type, they prefer to live their life the way they see fit. Both Aquarius types have a strong belief system. They will fight if a cause is right. They hate to be fenced in and don't deal with emotional types very well because they operate on an intellectual level. Many crave change. Life gets boring if everything stays the same. They like to change jobs every seven years and don't mind uprooting the entire family if they want to spread their wings in a new direction. The one thing that is common among most Aquarius is they are unique, sometimes unusual individuals. They are ahead of their time.

The best way to get a Water Bearer to leave is to be unwilling to make any changes. Refuse to go along with their game plan. Make them feel stifled and stuck. Moan, groan, and complain. Be the worst nag possible! Cut them off from their friends. Don't support their dreams and visions. Let them know you intend to stay put in the same house for the next fifty years, and expect them to do the same.

What to say to an Aquarius: "I forbid you to see your crazy friends ever again. They're jerks! You had better be willing to show me a lot more attention. I need an emotional lover! You're not as good in the sack as you think you are!"

How to Lose a Pisces

Pisces is one of the signs that refuses to let go. They hang on forever to dying relationships. Part of the problem is that they feel a lot of the issues really are their fault. They feel guilty when they shouldn't and are scared to be alone. The Fish is also very indecisive. Some are sensitive romantics. Others like to smother you. Nearly all are "whiners." Pisces' needs are very simple: they need to save you!

They enjoy being your knight in shining armor, the victim, the martyr. They thrive on constant drama.

How do you get this sign out of your life? It's going to be difficult. The easiest way is to pack your bags, drive away, and leave no forwarding address.

How to Attract Anyone to You

If you've escaped from "love prison" and parted ways with your cell mate, now it's time to look for your soul mate. I'll share a few astrological secrets on how to attract anyone. All you need to know is their zodiac sign!

The Aries Man

If a red-hot Aries man has caught your eye, don't act too anxious! Hide your attraction, but make sure he notices you. He is the biggest flirt in all the zodiac, so there's likely to be a throng of women admiring him, too. You must stand out in the crowd. Your Aries man likes a challenge as well as a good chase. If you're too easy, he'll lose interest. This is a guy who enjoys spontaneity, creative lovemaking, and a woman who can hold her own. If you're weepy, whiny, or indecisive, he'll lose patience. Be optimistic and ambitious. Let him put some effort into the relationship. He'll appreciate it more. Also, Aries are very competitive and like to be number one at everything. So once you've captured his heart, let him know he's the best lover ever, the most successful man you've ever met, and everything you've ever dreamed of.

The Aries Woman

In a relationship the Aries woman not only needs to know that she's number one in your life, she needs to "feel" it. This sassy, no-nonsense gal admires a strong man. Even though she tends to be a bit bossy and likes to take the lead in a relationship, the Aries woman will lose interest quickly if you give in to her whims all the time. She likes a challenge and a strong, assertive man. No wimps need apply for her affection. Do not take this woman for granted. If she feels neglected, she'll look elsewhere. She has lots of passion and craves excitement. Keep things lively and fun. And whatever you do, do not look at another woman.

Best Bets: Sagittarius, Leo, Gemini, Aquarius

Fast Fizzles: Cancer, Capricorn, Scorpio

Opposite Attraction: Libra

Past-Life Probability: Pisces

The Taurus Man

This down-to-earth man is hard to catch but easy to keep. It may take him a while to ask you out, but once he has his heart set on you, watch out. He won't let anything stand in his way to win your heart. He's very determined and patient. To win his undying devotion, you must be a real lady. Dress up when you go out. Make him work for a first kiss, and never sleep with a Taurus early on in a relationship. The way to a Taurus' heart is through his eyes and stomach, so invite him over for a home-cooked meal. Since Bulls are creatures of habit, schedule dinner every Sunday, and make Friday night your movie date. The more he develops a regular schedule and pattern with you, the less likely he is to change it.

Make him feel comfortable in your home. Never try to make him jealous. If a Taurus feels you are not faithful and a big flirt, they'll drop you like a hot potato.

The Taurus Woman

Consistency is a must in a relationship with a Taurus woman. Be on time and fulfill your promises. Don't break dates. Dress nicely and always look your best. Security is important when Taurus ladies are looking for love. You don't have to be a millionaire, but you should be able to support yourself, drive a decent vehicle, and afford a gourmet meal every now and then. Buy her chocolates and roses. Talk about the investments you are making and the money you're saving for the future. Like Taurus men, the women are just as jealous and possessive. Don't anger them, or you'll be sorry. Taurus women like peace and harmony. If you live a crazy lifestyle in constant chaos, this woman is not for you. A perfect date would be a walk in the woods, a bike ride, or an outdoor picnic. Being an earth sign, Taurus feel best when they're one with nature.

Best Bets: Cancer, Virgo, Capricorn, Pisces

Fast Fizzles: Leo, Aquarius

Opposite Attraction: Scorpio

Past-Life Probability: Aries

The Gemini Man

You'll need to be quick-witted, funny, and mentally stimulating to attract a Gemini man. He's a flirt and a little boy who refuses to grow up. You'll never be bored, but make sure he's doesn't get bored with you. You'll need to keep the fire sizzling hot! Get creative in the bedroom. Since a Gemini man is always changing his mind, you'll need to reinvent yourself. Be open to trying new adventures with him. Act silly. Play together. Ignore his moodiness. Remember he has two personalities, so you'll need to date them both! He may have ex-girlfriends who are now "just friends." Don't demand that he give them up too soon, or he'll give you the boot. Don't nag or give advice all the time. Let him talk. He will talk . . . a lot. Be a good listener. Let him be himself. Don't bring up commitment—let him do it. If he feels you're looking for "forever," he may run. Once a Gemini man feels you don't "need" him and are self-sufficient and stable, he's more likely to settle down. You can't allow the relationship to get boring.

The Gemini Woman

To entice a Gemini woman, you can't act macho, sexist, or egotistical. She wants a guy who is creative and fun loving, and can hold a conversation. You need to be a good listener because this lady will talk your ear off! A guy needs to be intellectual on some level to excite her. Write a heartfelt poem, or leave lots of love notes on her car windshield. Leave clever, enticing messages on her answering machine. If you're an animal lover, you get extra points! She adores puppies and kittens. Don't be possessive, because when a Gemini lady feels smothered, she'll run. Because Geminis change their mind a lot, be open to spur-of-the-moment changes. Be flexible with your schedule. Don't nag if she's late—she's always late! The best way to win the heart of a Gemini lady is to be her best friend first, someone she can talk to about anything.

Best Bets: Libra, Aquarius, Leo, Aries

Fast Fizzles: Pisces, Virgo

Opposite Attraction: Sagittarius

Past-Life Probability: Taurus

The Cancer Man

This man makes a good husband and father. He's very emotional and sensitive, so make sure you don't hurt his feelings. He's looking for a wife who reminds him of his mother. You must want to have children and be dedicated to making a comfortable home. To attract this kind of guy, don't be too bold. Be feminine. He'll admire you if you use a gentle touch rather than a flirtatious come-on. Talk about how much family tradition means to you. Be extra kind to his mom and get to know his friends. Do not flirt or talk about the men in your past. Even though he knows better, the Cancer man wants to think he's the only one you'll ever love. He doesn't want you to have a "past." Make him feel safe and secure. Tell him over and over you think he's great. He needs constant reassurance. Call when you say you will. Don't play games with him or play hard to get, or he'll feel rejected. When he gets moody, don't get mad or take it personally. Just reassure him that you think he's the greatest man in the whole wide world.

The Cancer Woman

Old boyfriends and ex-husbands will always attempt to come back into the Cancer's woman's life. It's because she's so maternal towards them. They felt loved and protected. If you want to win her heart, act like a real gentleman. Be romantic. If you're invited to her family's house for dinner, bring her flowers and a bouquet for her mother, too. Let her know she is the most beautiful woman you've ever dated. Cancers are not into moving in together. They're the marrying type. Let her know how important it is for you to settle down one day and have children. Fuss over her cooking. Compliment her figure. When she gets moody, hold her. Don't let full moons destroy the relationship. Cancers get irrational when there's a full moon and are very sensitive over the least little things. Tell her often how much you love her. Buy her mushy cards for no reason and teddy bears to decorate her room. Never, ever forget her birthday.

Best Bets: Taurus, Scorpio, Virgo, Pisces

Fast Fizzles: Aquarius, Aries, Libra

Opposite Attraction: Capricorn

Past-Life Probability: Gemini

The Leo Man

Both the male and female Lions are known to have the most generous hearts of all the zodiac. They give 110 percent in a relationship, but if they feel neglected, Leos become sourpusses. The way to attract a Leo man is to make a fuss over him. Admire him. Praise him. Tell him how wonderful he is. Listen to him talk about himself. Put him on a pedestal and let him take the lead. Leos are very proud people and really care what others think of them. Their reputation is important. Look your best and dress well. Be charming and witty but don't hog his spotlight. He wants the attention focused on him. Best advice? Appreciate him. Let him know how thankful you are for everything he does for you. Show him lots of love and affection—you'll get it back threefold.

The Leo Woman

The Lioness wants and expects to be treated like a princess. Don't be cheap when taking her out on the town. Avoid cheesy buffet lines. Opt for at least one fine dining experience a week. Buy her little presents and tell her she's the most beautiful woman you've ever laid eyes on. Hint: gifts made of gold or that sparkle win you extra points. She is looking for a man who is successful and charming. You don't need to be as wealthy as Donald Trump, but she will expect you to have enough funds to pamper her. Get to know and appreciate her friends. Be supportive of her career, and encourage her dreams and goals. Take her to exotic places. This lady could be high maintenance but worth her weight in gold to the man who appreciates her.

Best Bets: Sagittarius, Gemini, Libra, Aries

Fast Fizzles: Scorpio, Taurus

Opposite Attraction: Aquarius

Past-Life Probability: Cancer

The Virgo Man

Mr. Virgo is no doubt a perfectionist, so you need to be on your very best behavior when you're initially introduced. First impressions count, and this man will look you over to make sure there are no flaws. Are you intimidated yet? If you are, move on to another sign. If you like a challenge, read on! Virgo loves an intellectual woman, one who can carry on a sensible conversation. He has no patience with ditsy airheads. Show him your intelligent side on the first date, your warm and bubbly personality on the second, and maybe your sexy side by the third. But don't come on too strong. Virgos are not called the "virgins" for nothing, you know! They're not prudes but are respectable. Other words of wisdom if you're trying to attract such a man: keep your car immaculate and your house clean. They are fussy and nitpicky, and hate clutter and dirt. Be a little needy because these guys love to be needed. They enjoy fixing things for you or helping out. So come up with a few ways they can be helpful.

The Virgo Woman

Like her male counterpart, the Virgo woman is particular about how her partner looks. She only finds certain "types" attractive. Sometimes these gals seem to draw all the bad boys, whose lives they are trying to save. Then they hang on to these relationships, long past their prime, in hopes their partner will change. So, if you have a record, are unemployed, or need immediate help, you have a decent chance at getting to know a Virgo lady! All kidding aside, these gals appreciate a man with good taste, someone who is a gentleman and knows how to treat a woman. They desperately hope that chivalry isn't dead. Prove to them it is alive by being the best, most attentive date ever. Don't ever let her catch you cussing up a storm or whistling at other women. The most important thing to remember is that it's the little details that count with a Virgo woman. Remembering her favorite restaurant and how to mix her drink just right, and slipping little love notes on her pillow when she's not looking will win you points.

Best Bets: Taurus, Capricorn, Scorpio, Cancer

Fast Fizzles: Gemini, Sagittarius

Opposite Attraction: Pisces

Past-Life Probability: Leo

The Libra Man

Libra men have a grand idea of what their future mate is supposed to represent. In reality, no one is likely to match his ideal, but if you have your heart set on a Libra guy, go ahead and give it your best shot. Always look your very best. Look feminine and be charming. But don't be afraid to take the lead in the relationship because sometimes this man likes it that way. Let him know you play fair. Don't create chaos in his life. Keep things peaceful and harmonious. Understand that he will change his mind about a commitment many times. Your patience will pay off as a Libra man can be the most romantic and attentive partner you'll ever have.

The Libra Woman

The Libra woman loves romance. In fact, to her, love is what life is all about. Be attentive and caring. Indulge her with lovely little gifts and enchanted evenings. Take a walk in the moonlight. Bring her pink roses and candy. Never swear or lose your temper. Libras like peace. They hate vulgarity. You will need to create a balance in your relationship once it is established or she could smother and mother you to death. Friendships and her social circle are important to her, so be nice to those she cares about. Libras have an appreciation for the finer things in life. Art, music, and nature are appealing to her. So is poetry, so make sure you always sign the little love cards you give her with a poetic note about how much you adore her. She'll treasure any memento you give her. Romance is what she lives for.

Best Bets: Gemini, Leo, Aquarius, Sagittarius

Fast Fizzles: Capricorn, Cancer

Opposite Attraction: Aries

Past-Life Probability: Virgo

The Scorpio Man

This guy appears laid-back and easygoing, as if he wouldn't hurt a fly. But guess again. Beneath his cool, calm exterior lies a deep intensity and passion that can't be matched by any other sign of the zodiac. You need to earn his trust. It may take some time because Scorpio trusts no one. Consistency is the key. Scorpio men need their women to be sexy, down-to-earth, and a little bit of a challenge. The Scorpio man is intuitive, so don't lie or manipulate him. He'll catch on right away. Be considerate of his feelings, but don't allow him to walk all over yours. His moodiness could drive you a little mad, but his other qualities will make up for the mood swings. Don't attempt to make him jealous. He is paranoid anyway and smells evil even when it doesn't exist. Plus, he'll feel you're untrustworthy. He likes to feel safe and in control in a relationship. After time, your Scorpio man will be a loyal, loving, and devoted mate (as long as he thinks he's getting his way).

The Scorpio Woman

If you really want to get to know a Scorpio woman, practice patience and perseverance. She, like her male counterpart, needs to trust you completely before she commits. Make sure you are up to the challenge because this lady is like no one you've ever met. Be honest, because she'll know if you're lying. Be attentive and on time. If you make a promise, keep it. Scorpios don't forget anything. The Scorpio woman is sensitive but doesn't always show it. Her poker face will never reveal if she's really interested in you. But once you seduce her (or she seduces you), you'll know for sure where this intense woman stands. For most Scorpio women, a good sex life is important. All the rumors you've heard about their sexual appetite are true, so make sure you can keep up with her! Once she feels safe with you, she will be an extremely loyal and committed partner. She needs to have control at all times, but she loses interest in wimps. So you must walk a fine line between being strong and willing to bend.

Best Bets: Cancer, Pisces, Capricorn, Virgo

Fast Fizzles: Leo, Aquarius

Opposite Attraction: Taurus

Past-Life Probability: Libra

The Sagittarius Man

The Sagittarius man is like a little boy who will never grow up! He makes you feel like a princess when you're with him, but understand that no one will ever tie him down. The way to catch these career bachelors is to first and foremost be their best friend. Join in on the activities he prefers. Don't ever talk about commitment or the future. Let him bring it up, and when he does, don't act overanxious. Keep your relationship interesting. If you let things fall into a rut, the Sagittarius man will look for greener pastures. Try to always be upbeat, positive, and ready to change your schedule at the last minute, without complaining. Sag men hate naggers. They don't want to feel fenced in. They prefer women who are independent, can roll with the punches, and aren't the jealous type. Ex-girlfriends will call him, so make sure you're confident enough within yourself to handle the attention Prince Charming will receive.

The Sagittarius Woman

The Sagittarius woman likes her independence. She is honest and direct and seldom takes tips from Martha Stewart. To woo an Archer woman, you must be someone who will bring more excitement into her life. She already has tons of friends and a hectic schedule. She needs someone who can "add" something to her life. You must share in her passion as well. Being athletic is a plus, because this gal has a sporty side, too. If you look hot in a pair of blue jeans and a crisp white T-shirt, you'll get extra points. Keep your complaints and your anti-depression pills to yourself. This lady looks at everything in a positive light. Ms. Sagittarius is looking for a lover, a best friend, and a confidante all wrapped up into one package. Don't ever make her feel trapped, attempt to smother her, or tell her what she's going to do and when. She'll bolt for the nearest exit. Keep her laughing. A sense of humor goes a long way with this lady.

Best Bets: Leo, Aries, Libra, Aquarius

Fast Fizzles: Pisces, Virgo, Cancer

Opposite Attraction: Gemini

Past-Life Probability: Scorpio

The Capricorn Man

The Capricorn man is the strong silent type, but beneath his cool exterior is a man who really wants to find the "perfect" woman and fall in love. To be that woman, you should act very ladylike and a bit conservative. Show him that you are traditional and loyal. Expecting the best of yourself will make you shine in his eyes all the more. Allow him to be the "man" in the relationship, but don't let him get away with bossing you around. Capricorns like to be in charge. Know that he's serious and not as emotional as other zodiac signs. Don't pressure him to talk about his feelings. Sometimes he appears cheap, though he thinks of himself as thrifty and a good saver. He's a logical man. He probably has a strong work ethic, so encourage and support his career goals. Gain his trust and respect, and the rest will be easy. He's looking for a long-term commitment. Even though he is cautious about letting his heart get the best of him, he does want marriage and the white picket fence one day.

The Capricorn Woman

She's a no-nonsense, manner-of-fact, businesswoman who knows what she wants and goes after it. She's down-to-earth and can be extremely cautious about getting involved with someone. But once a Capricorn woman falls in love, it's usually for keeps. She appreciates the nicer things in life, and her standards are very high. You'll have to prove yourself to her over and over again, but it's worth the effort because Capricorn women are loyal and dependable. If you want a sexual relationship with her, this lady wants to know that you are seriously looking toward a future with her. Control your temper. Don't swear a lot. Make a decent income. Be honest. Talk about your plans for the future and how you intend to be financially secure. Stick to a schedule and routine. Be consistent and try to be as organized as you possibly can. That about wraps up what a Capricorn gal wants in man. If you're a mess, a drunk, unemployed, or have a lot of "baggage" from past relationships, you don't stand a chance with this woman.

Best Bets: Taurus, Virgo, Scorpio

Fast Fizzles: Libra, Aries, Gemini

Opposite Attraction: Cancer

Past-Life Probability: Sagittarius

The Aquarius Man

The Aquarius man is a "know-it-all." He is intelligent and has an opinion on everything. If you want to win his heart, let him talk and make him feel what he has to say is very important. Here's a guy who appreciates his freedom, so don't pressure him into a commitment or be overly demanding of his time. There are two types of Aquarius men: extroverted and introverted. If yours is friendly and outgoing, you may have to compete for his time and attention with the many friends he has. Join in the group and learn to like his quirky buddies. If he's the quiet type, give him his space when he needs it. You must be willing to make changes in your life, with both types of men. Be willing to try new adventures like sky diving or mountain climbing. Did you know you're interested in a computer genius? Better make sure you have an e-mail address so the two of you can communicate more often. The Aquarius man is known to spend hours online. He's a man's man, so don't do anything that would make him look foolish, feminine, or less than the macho guy he is! He hates being told what to do. Be kind, gentle, and a little bit of a risk taker yourself, and you could find a love match.

The Aquarius Woman

The Aquarius woman is a free spirit and devoted to her causes and friends. If she can fit you in her busy schedule, great! If not, you'll have to prove yourself worthy of her precious time. The best way to woo her is to be her friend first. Have conversations about astrology, the world, relationships, and deep topics. She'll be direct with her words, so don't mince yours. She likes a strong, self-assured man with a tender side. Show her both. She craves change, so whatever you do, don't get stuck in a boring dating routine. Make sure to liven things up every other weekend. Try new things. Take her to places she's never been before. Don't be passive or jealous. Forget mind games and playing hard to get. Honesty with an Aquarius woman is always the best policy. Keep things interesting. Surprise her. She's not into money as much as she's into security and honesty. If this Aquarius woman can talk to you about anything, if she feels you're her very best friend, and if she mentions making plans for the holidays that include you, you probably have conquered her heart!

Best Bets: Gemini, Libra, Sagittarius, Aries

Fast Fizzles: Cancer, Taurus, Scorpio

Opposite Attraction: Leo

Past-Life Probability: Capricorn

The Pisces Man

The Pisces man can be the most romantic guy you've ever met—or the most utterly impossible. Pisces men at their best are kind, gentle, intuitive, and dreamy. At their worst they drink too much, constantly whine, and get depressed a lot. If you've already fallen head over heels for a Fish, here's what you do: get romantic, too. Spend hours with him making memories in and outside of the bedroom. Plan a special weekend at a bed and breakfast near a lake. Watch sunsets together. Talk about his dreams and fantasies. Be his cheerleader in life but not his "enabler" or addiction. Bring some structure into his world, for he needs it badly. Make plans and schedules, and stick to them. Let him know you'll be there through thick and thin. Be someone he can depend on. He may try to smother you. If you like your independence, you may have to give up a little private time for yourself to please him.

The Pisces Woman

The Pisces lady loves to please! The needier you are, the better! She loves to feel as if she is your "everything." She will stick by you through whatever comes your way. A Pisces woman is very psychic yet sometimes very insecure, so you must make her always feel safe and emotionally secure in a relationship. She'll remember all the little things you do for her, so write her a love letter, buy her a rose, or give her a box of candy to delight her sweet tooth. She loves romance and probably has been dreaming of Prince Charming all her life. Be her knight in shining armor, someone she can lean on and share her fears and sorrows with. She's been searching for her soul mate for years. Discover your past lives together. Take her to romantic, weepy movies. Find a breathtaking view at a park, waterfall, or mountainside that she can call "our special place." Anything you do to romance this lady will win you points. She's not interested in money as much as she is interested in your heart. Make her feel like a princess. Any effort you put forth to make this relationship magical and special will be returned threefold through her devotion and love.

Best Bets: Cancer, Scorpio, Taurus, Capricorn

Fast Fizzles: Gemini, Sagittarius

Opposite Attraction: Virgo

Past-Life Probability: Aquarius

When lookin' for love, you'll want to harness as much positive energy from the universe as you can, and that means timing is everything. Many of you probably get your tarot cards read or your astrology chart run at least once a year. Have you ever considered numerology? Numbers have power and different meanings. Your birth day numbers can reveal your future. In the next chapter I'd like to share with you a numerology formula you can learn easily and always have at your fingertips. It will help you predict the next nine years of your love life!

Maria Shaw's Predictive Numerology

You discovered your birth number and the personality traits associated with it in chapter 6. Now let's look at predictive numerology. I've designed my own numerology formula to help you predict the next nine years of your life. This is a simple formula that's easy to learn. You'll amaze your family and friends when you do a reading for them. I've used this method for thousands of clients over the past ten years, and it has never failed.

In this numerology formula, our lives run in nine-year cycles. Each cycle has a different meaning. We deal with different issues and the emphasis is placed on a certain path in our life each year. The cycle runs from birthday to birthday rather than calendar year to calendar year. This is important to remember. I will explain the different cycles shortly.

Your Numerology Number for the Year

Here's the formula to calculate your numerology number for the year.

1. Take your birth month, and add it to your day of birth (do *not* include the year).
   Example: June 4 = 6 + 4 = 10

2. This is the tricky part: Add the above number to the current year master number. Let's use the master year for 2005, which is 43, as you can see in the following chart.

Current Year Master Number

   2004 – 42

   2005 – 43

   2006 – 44

   2007 – 45

   2008 – 46

   2009 – 47

   2010 – 48

   So, 10 + 43 (master number for 2005) = 53

3. Reduce that last number to a single digit.
   53 = 5 + 3 = 8

4. Your numerology number for the year is 8.

It is extremely important to remember that this numerology formula does not run from calendar year to calendar year. It runs from your birth date to your next birth date.

For example, if your next birthday falls on December 31, 2005, you cannot use the master number for 2005 until you reach your birthday. You will still be working off the 2004 master number until the end of 2005. If your birthday is April 1, 2005, you will be working off the 2004 master number for the first four months of 2005. Then in April, begin using the 2005 master number.

Numerology Cycles

#1 Year

This is a year of bright, beautiful beginnings. The emphasis is on *you!* Your needs, wishes, and dreams will be the focus. I always tell my clients, when you are in your number-one year, you can get *anything* you want, but you need to ask for it. No one is going to hand you anything on a silver platter. You may have to ask more than once for your heart's desire, but it's likely that you will receive it. Anyone coming into a number-one year should take the time to make a wish list. This is most effective when done on your actual birthday. The list should include everything you want, big and small. It doesn't matter if some of the things sound silly. Just write them down. This is *your* year. I recall a friend of my mine who put a new boyfriend at the top of her list on her June birthday. By October she was in a relationship with a great guy! But make sure when you make your list that you are very specific. If you were to write that you want to meet a guy, you could attract all of the bums in town. Write something like this: "I want to meet a nice, polite, honest, hard-working, handsome guy who has similar interests."

#2 Year

The number-two cycle is one of the bigger relationship years. It's not necessarily a romantic time. It's more apt to be time of reflection on individual needs in a relationship. If all your friends are dating, you will want to find a special someone, too. Any problems or issues that come up in a relationship can easily be addressed and resolved now. Love seems to be flowing through everyone you meet in the number-two year. This is a year when many people "rediscover" love in a long-term commitment, appreciate one another more, or meet someone new and fall madly in love! One thing is for sure: in a number-two year, you are very aware of your own needs in a relationship—what you are willing to put up with and what you're not. You will not settle for less than what your heart desires!

#3 Year

Communication, travel, and creative pursuits fill the number-three cycle. You won't feel much like hanging out alone. You'll want to hit the open road (you may get a new car, too), and your social life will be in full swing. There will be lots of parties and special events to attend. New and long-lasting friendships could develop. Any clubs or organizations you join will benefit you greatly. Let the good times roll! This is a time for schmoozing, making new contacts, and enjoying life. Have all the fun you can handle now because when your number-four year rolls around, there won't be time as the focus will be on work. So where are you going to meet someone special? Obviously, because you are quite the social butterfly now, look anywhere where the people are! Also, a friendship with the opposite sex could turn into something more this year. Look among your close circle of friends for romantic attractions, too. When traveling, either near or far from home, there's a good chance for romance as you'll meet lots of friendly new people.

#4 Year

This will be the best year for your career in over nine years, so you'll want to make the most of it. Unfortunately, that could mean that your love life will have to take a back seat now. You'll have to work hard at balancing career responsibilities and making time for your honey. If you're single, it may be harder to meet people, so where are you most likely to find love? Perhaps around the water cooler at the office, or somewhere on the job front. It could be a client you meet who sets your heart aflutter. It could be the guy or gal who sits next to you. It could even be your boss! Work-related events like business conferences and office parties are also favorable to make contacts that will prove valuable to your success during this cycle. You could increase your income, too. If you do make more money, it will be through your own hard work.

#5 Year

This is the year to fall madly in love! It's a time when you will have lots of options and many dating opportunities! It will seem as if men (or women) are coming out of the woodwork. Where have they been all these years? you ask yourself. If you're a guy who hasn't had much luck with the ladies, this is your year to turn that trend around! Know that you will not like everyone you meet. There will be a few losers chasing after you. Keep your running shoes handy! But at least one person will be a keeper, and in fact you could be dating several people at one time. Among the guys and gals you meet in the number-five year could be a special someone with whom you may walk down the aisle in your number-seven year (the marriage year). The number-five year is also a time in which you may move, relocate, or redecorate your home. Your libido hits an all-time high and you exude lots of sex appeal. The number-five year is also a pregnancy year. No wonder! If you're single, make sure you get out of the house and meet new people. I always tell my clients that by staying home, you won't meet a soul except the pizza delivery man! If you're married, you can recapture lots of passion with your mate, but be careful—it is also the year of the "illicit affair"!

#6 Year

The number-six cycle is a year in which you feel a strong desire to get your life in order. If you're not happy with your current relationship, you'll work to improve it, get into counseling, or leave it altogether. If you hate your job, you'll look for another one. It's one of the best times to overcome a bad habit, quit smoking, lose weight, or clean out your closets. Anything you want to do, you have the determination and willpower to see it through. I call the number-six year the discipline year. It can be very boring at times, but it is a great year for change. Many people end negative relationships during this cycle. If you're single and want to meet someone, get yourself emotionally and spiritually in shape before you enter the dating field. Then after that you can draw healthy people to you much more easily. You may meet like-minded people at the gym while you're working on losing that weight. This isn't a big cycle for meeting new lovers as much as it is dumping the old ones or working out issues in therapy.

#7 Year

This is the "legal year." Many people get married, engaged, divorced, buy property, or sign legal papers during the seven cycle. It is also a very spiritual year, so you could become enlightened to the law of love and meet your soul mate! Many people also find themselves in court, and they actually do pretty well during this time with any legal affairs. If you're fighting a traffic ticket or hoping to sue someone for a million bucks, do it in your number-seven year because your chances of winning are better. The odds are in your favor. You could get more recognition than ever before on the job and may receive some sort of award, too. If you were unhappy in a marriage in your number-six year but didn't file for divorce, you could so in the number-seven year. If you met someone special in your number-five year, you could be making wedding plans this year. It's a great time to get psychic or astrology readings, go back to school, and invest money. But as for love, it's all or nothing this year!

#8 Year

This is an excellent money year. The number-eight year brings money to you effortlessly. Financial rewards do not always have to come via the job front. Expensive gifts, clothes, and trips could come your way. Since you will have more money at your disposal, you could invest in hobbies or other interests. This is a great time to ask for a raise at work or see your investments pay off. Good deals and bargains are easily found. Just don't think this trend is going to last forever. Stash some of your cash for a rainy day. In regard to love, you may meet someone very wealthy or at the very least someone who wants to shower you with gifts and lavish dates. If married, your spouse could make more money. The cash flow may not always be consistent, but by tax time next year you'll see that your income has definitely increased.

#9 Year

This year wraps up your entire nine-year cycle. Here, we deal with the karma of the past eight years—in other words, lessons you still need to learn or debts you need to repay. Anything you didn't do or handle correctly in the previous cycles, you must address now. You have no choice. Some people fear the approaching nine year. Others are not affected by it at all because they have lived their cycles correctly. Many times the past will come back to haunt you. For instance, if you ended a relationship badly with your ex, you'll probably meet up to make amends. Your number-nine year doesn't always bring bad luck, but most of us don't always follow the straight and narrow. There are usually some things we must contend with. The least you will experience is a feeling of being "held back." It's as if you can't get ahead, no matter how hard you push. The universe is telling you to slow down. Allow yourself time to reflect. You'll be up and running when the number-one year hits on your next birthday. In regard to love, there may be an ending. If you didn't end a bad relationship in the number six or seven cycle, it will likely come to an end now. People from your past will come back into your life, some unexpectedly, if you still have issues with them. If you're still in love with someone and you want to "try" again, the number-nine year can afford you that very opportunity!

Sun Sign Compatibility Guide

If you still need more ammunition in your quest for your soul mate, here's a little *lagniappe*, as we say in New Orleans, a little something extra—a complete sun sign compatibility chapter. There are over 144 combinations. You should also take into consideration a person's entire astrological chart when deciding compatibility between two people. This would include the rising sign, moon sign, Venus, and Mars. For the sake of keeping things simple for all readers, it will be sufficient to read your sun sign, and your rising sign if you know it. Your rising sign is very important and can be obtained by getting a natal chart done by a professional astrologer. These days, you can likely find the information on the internet.

If you know your love interest's birth date, you can make a more informed decision whether to further a relationship or not. If you're currently in a commitment, this chapter can help you understand the weaknesses and strengths of the relationship. I believe you can make any relationship work if you have a real understanding of your lover's personality and know what makes them "tick." Of course, there are signs that get along with one another much more easily than others. But in any situation, general knowledge about the sun sign can help a great deal in making relationships work.

♈

Aries: The Ram
(March 21–April 21)

Aries with Aries

This could be a decent match if they let each other take turns being the leader. The biggest problems arise when both of them want to be in charge. These two hotheads will create the quarrels of the century. Know that passionate energy can also be used in sustaining a long-term commitment.

Aries with Taurus

This could be a good sexual relationship and at times could be financially rewarding (especially for the Aries). But a long-term commitment could spell disaster. Taurus are slow. They think things through. They save money. They enjoy the comforts of home and basically do not favor change. Aries are always throwing caution to the wind, spending money spontaneously. They thrive on change, the newness of life. Many times, Aries do not think before they act. Taurus' need for emotional and financial security may not always agree with Aries' pioneering and independent attitude. Taurus can be extremely stubborn and cannot be pushed. Aries will learn patience from the Bull, but eventually will refuse to use it.

Aries with Gemini

Here are two quick-witted signs who love to talk. Aries love to talk about themselves. Geminis love to talk about everything and anything. It is the one sign that finds it very hard not to communicate. Aries and Gemini will explore similar interests, including travel, movies, and higher intellectual pursuits. Even arguing can be fun for these two. Gemini is just as quick as the Aries with the comebacks and, don't be fooled, just as direct! Love can grow here. This is one of the better combinations. Both Aries and Gemini embrace change. They can't stand to be bored. These are the couples that go skydiving on their first date, whitewater rafting on their second, and on a Las Vegas honeymoon on their third! So move out of their way and watch what happens. More often than not, their relationship will blossom quickly, grow, and endure.

Aries with Cancer

The initial sexual attraction between the Ram and the Crab is like a magnet! But watch out. We're mixing fire and water here. After the first few weeks, the whirlwind romance loses momentum, and it's all downhill from there. Cancer wants home and family, plus a mate who is on time for dinner, is there when they need a shoulder to cry on and, most importantly, is someone they can nest with. But Aries has friends expecting them, places to go, people to see. Cancer feels rejected, hurt, and abandoned. Aries cannot fathom Cancer's deep emotional and security needs. This relationship is going to require work, and I do mean hard work, if it's going to last. On the positive side, Cancer can provide a strong home base for the Aries when they must deal with any harsh realities of the world. Aries can show the moon children the optimistic side of the world when they get a little too crabby!

Aries with Leo

These two signs are born leaders. Both aggressive, these signs complement one another. There could be a bit of competition, but it will likely prove to be invigorating. Romance and love will be highlighted. There will be satin sheets and scented candles mixed with sexual spontaneity. They will need to curb their spending enthusiasm and extravagance, but this couple will enjoy life and push it to the limit. Careers and social status will be very important in the union, as well as friends, parties, and hobbies. If Aries and Leo can put their own egos aside and work from the soul level, this could be a dynamite combination.

Aries with Virgo

Aries are too headstrong and impatient to listen to Virgos nitpick, analyze, and criticize. Virgos want everything perfect and will do all they can to "help" Aries become just that. The problem lies within the fact the Aries already thinks—excuse me—"knows" they are perfect. Thus, the Aries will look at the Virgo's helpful suggestions as nagging. The initial stage of romance seems grand, but as time drags on, the relationship wears thin. These two are not on the same wavelength.

Aries could use their sense of humor to keep things going for a while. But the same old issues keep coming back. Virgo needs to be needed. After all, they are here to serve. But Aries' ideas of servitude could be strictly one-sided, leaving the Virgo feeling unappreciated.

Aries with Libra

They say opposites attract, and this certainly holds true for this fire/air combination. The Aries likes to lead, and the Libra will allow it. This pairing usually works well and is considered to have long-lasting qualities. Both of these signs know how to flirt, Aries in an aggressive Martian way and Libra in a subtle Venusian style. Libras enjoy peace and harmony. They desire it so much that they will usually give in to an argument for the sake of keeping the peace. So Aries learns they can keep pushing. If Aries doesn't learn to see Libra's side and makes no attempt to keep the relationship balanced, the Aries may just push Libra right out the door! For the most part, this couple can make it. Remember, Aries, do not take your partner for granted. And Libra, it's okay to speak up now and then. The Aries will respect and admire you all the more for it.

Aries with Scorpio

There is no way Scorpio is going to allow Aries to flirt outrageously and carry on in their usual manner unless, of course, it's between their own sheets. Aries will be deeply attracted to Scorpio's mysterious and sensual personality. Aries will enjoy the chase immensely but have regrets after the capture. They will find nothing gets past the Scorpio. There will be many emotional blowups, power battles, and so on. Scorpio will win, even to their own detriment. A Scorpio will force the Aries native to dig deep and look at their emotional side, and that could scare the Ram. The way Aries and Scorpio look at life is different, too, especially concerning sex. I would suggest a working or business relationship, but love is going to feel like a wild roller coaster ride, with Scorpio in charge of the on/off switch.

Aries with Sagittarius

The Aries/Sag combo can work because both parties are usually quite optimistic about life. This is the case where friends can become lovers. The two click in body and mind. They can sit and talk for hours. There is much satisfaction and encouragement between the Ram and the Archer. The downside is they could get in over their heads with their big ideas. Watch out for bankruptcy court rather than divorce court! This couple could enjoy travel to foreign lands. They'll encourage one another to achieve educational and career goals. They both like to live fast and seize the moment. If it gets dull, they know when to part, and can still remain friends long after the fire has gone out.

Aries with Capricorn

Capricorns play by the rules. They want a traditional, sometimes old-fashioned lifestyle. Aries are into trying anything new. Breaking rules is part of their pioneering spirit. So we have the past battling with the future. If these two could ever meet in the middle, a relationship just may work. But Capricorn is the sign of the Goat. They won't budge easily. These folks have strong, deeply imbedded opinions. Aries wants and needs to lead. The initial sexual attraction is strong, but the long-term probability is weak. This combination is good for career, but caution is advised for anything more than just a lustful look.

Aries with Aquarius

These lovers have just plain fun together—in work or play. They could create things. Together, they could work on teaching and sharing their talents with the universe. They motivate one another. In a love affair, this combination works in harmony as long as Aries truly sees the Water Bearer's vision and allows them the freedom to pursue their dreams. Aquarius will help Aries expand their intellectual curiosities about the New Age. These two signs are not mushy types but can be sensual and passionate. True friendships have been formed between Aries and Aquarius, and I have seen many marriages succeed with this combination of fire and air.

Aries with Pisces

The water of Pisces could easily put the fire of Aries out. Aries gets all excited about a new project, and Pisces immediately dampens the enthusiasm by pointing out the pitfalls. There is one connection between these two, and I'm not so sure it's a healthy one. Pisces tend to sacrifice for their mates. They put them on a pedestal. Sometimes they take on all of their partner's problems. Aries, as we know, love to sit right there at the top of that pedestal. They don't mind one bit if they are on the receiving end. This could easily become a one-sided relationship as long as Pisces plays their martyr role so well. Aries could lose interest after a while and go looking elsewhere. I suggest a "just friends" approach from the get-go.

Taurus: The Bull
(April 21–May 21)

Taurus with Taurus

Taurus men are all man, and Taurus women are very feminine. These two have the same needs: financial and emotional security. This usually works better than other same-sign partnerships. But at times, these two can be like a couple of old war horses not budging on issues and clashing in major power struggles. Jealousies can easily arise, but think of the money to be made! The biggest question of all is who will hold the checkbook?

Taurus with Gemini

I have seen this partnership work effectively with my parents. They were married for over fifty years. The steady, secure Bull helps ground the youthful Gemini. Taurus offers stability so Gemini can play and pursue their goals in life. The Bull says that's just fine as long as the Twin can show them the money. This is one combination in which money is easily produced, and working together seems to work. There are differences in how each perceives spending and saving. Love grows deeper over time. Crisis makes these couples more committed. It doesn't always work, but it has a better chance than other earth/air combinations.

Taurus with Cancer

This combination is usually a keeper. It is one of the best matches in all of the zodiac. Both are homebodies. Both need financial security. Both are loving, affectionate, committed people who marry for life. However, Taurus can be too unyielding and set in their ways for Cancer, who enjoys bossing people around. Any type of criticism will send Cancer into tears, and they will remember everything you said, the date, time, and place of the offense, and will make sure to bring it up years later, if needed. Cancer, you must learn not to take things too personally and just remember that the old Bull is never going to leave you. You're stuck, but you probably like it that way.

Taurus with Leo

Here's a combination that you always hear doesn't work. That's mostly true. But in my practice, I have found, surprisingly, that many of these Taurus/Leo marriages work. I have noted that in all of the successful marriages, both parties worked long hours, ran their own businesses, or were so committed to climbing the career ladder that they had no energy left to argue about anything. In general, Leos can be a little too dramatic and flashy for the down-to-earth Taurus. And those couples that do take the time to fight . . . well, it's a lion against a bull, and everyone knows a Leo will not give up the crown. Both signs need to know they are truly loved, and if the ego/power struggles in this relationship are too great, both parties will be left feeling empty.

Taurus with Virgo

This is a nice combination; two earth signs who appreciate the value of a dollar. Virgos are known to be the best shoppers, and Taurus can trust that their money is not being spent foolishly. Their needs are not extravagant, and they enjoy each other's company. Taurus loves to be pampered, and Virgo loves to be helpful and kind. So they are on the same page. There may be problems, however, when it comes to diet and health. Taurus loves to eat. It is one pleasure in life they will not be denied! Virgo worries about their health and everybody else's. If the Virgo is a health nut and is the household cook, Taurus will be left unsatisfied. But if this is the only disagreement these two have, then not to worry—there's always take-out.

Taurus with Libra

Both Taurus and Libra are ruled by the planet Venus, so there will initially be a mutual understanding and attraction between these two signs. However, Venus works differently in each sign, and Libra's love of friends and spur-of-the-moment parties will not go over well with Taurus' well-planned routine. The physical desire is there, but for a long-term commitment there could be problems with possessiveness on the Bull's part. Libra won't be tied down too long. They will bend only so far to keep the peace, and then they leave. The Taurus has a habit of becoming too condescending in this relationship if things don't go their way. But this comes from insecurity rather than anything else. They are afraid of losing the Libra to their friends or other VIPs.

Taurus with Scorpio

Hot, hot, hot! Take the best sex sign in the zodiac, Scorpio, and place them with the stamina and sensuality of Taurus the Bull, and you can't get a better combination for erotica. But watch out—the fires don't just start in the bedroom. This could be an endearing, long-lasting relationship or the most dangerous one these two will likely encounter in one lifetime. One thing is for sure: if they part ways, they both will look at love in a completely different way. This is the type of relationship that is either very good or very bad. There is no in-between. I think the longer the Scorpio and the Bull stay together, the more challenges they will meet. In turn, their bond grows stronger and then nothing can break these two apart. The key is to forget about who has the upper hand, and just go for it.

Taurus with Sagittarius

I don't find this combination very often. It is a good financial part-nership. The Sag will help the Bull look at things from a different perspective, and perhaps teach them about new religions, philoso-phies, and foreign places, and maybe even about love. However, Taurus the Bull could stomp on Sagittarius' freedom-loving ways. This will leave the Archer feeling suffocated and smothered, which, for a Sagittarius, is a fate worse than death! I don't see how this re-lationship can experience longevity. The Sag will eventually break free if the Taurus doesn't change. But that's not in the Bull's nature or in their best interest, so leave this pairing for business and money-making ventures only.

Taurus with Capricorn

These two earth creatures can see eye to eye on most things. I'm not so sure the sexual excitement will be as strong between these two as with other couples, but there is a deeper agreement when it comes to how life should be lived. The two share a strong work ethic and will save money for old age. At times the relationship may seem dull, but I don't foresee either one leaving on that account. No, it would have to be a major faux pas—infidelity, abandonment, or a secret bank account the other partner knew nothing about.

Taurus with Aquarius

This is a crazy combination. There will be many ups and downs caused by a lack of understanding of one another's personality type and basic needs. Taurus needs to possess, to feel secure, to stay with the known. Aquarius needs change. They crave it. It's almost as if they need change in order to survive. In the beginning of such a relationship, the Taurus may go along with trying the new things the Aquarius introduces. It could as simple as foreign food, travel, or New Age ideas. But the longer the relationship goes on, the more strongly the Bull will resist the new concepts, and Aquarius will find themselves fighting to keep their true identity and wondering what went wrong. The Bull will gently nudge the Water Bearer back into their world, and the cycle will start all over again. Sometimes this match works if the Taurus allows the Aquarius the variety and change they need. The Taurus may not always agree or understand the Aquarius' unusual ways, but in order for such a relationship to last, the Bull has to at least accept them if they can not embrace them.

Taurus with Pisces

Pisces can add a bit of magic to a Taurus' everyday world. They turn an ordinary day into a mystical journey. The practical Taurus seldom allows themselves to get caught up in the fairy tale of life. Pisces will help Taurus experience the joy of escaping for a while, through meditation, art, music, wine, massage, and daydreaming. Taurus will usually find this exhilarating. They keep Pisces from going too far with escapism by helping bring them back down to earth, gently reminding them of the daily basic chores and lessons: security, money, home, and family. This earth/water combination can do well if they learn to take the best of both signs and blend the spiritual and practical sides together.

Taurus with Aries

After they get done deciding who's going to take the lead, these two could get much accomplished. For long-term love, however, there is much more needed to sustain this union. Taurus will not be pushed, bribed, or shoved into anything they don't want to be. Aries just may be too impatient to wait for the old Bull to come to their senses. The fire could go out rather quickly for an Aries waiting for the Taurus to light up. I would rethink this one.

♊

Gemini: The Twins
(May 21–June 21)

Gemini with Gemini

This combination is like living with four people! Putting two Twins together may be too much. There will be plenty to talk about, but if no one is doing the listening, there are bound to be problems. This could still work, although personally I feel the whole relationship could be a little overwhelming. I suggest taking turns, working as hard as you play at the relationship, and keeping "the evil one" in check. It could be worse. You could end up with someone who doesn't communicate.

Gemini with Cancer

This is an excellent combination for boyfriend/girlfriend relationships. But a walk down the aisle would need to be reconsidered. Cancer would likely take on the role of mother to the young-at-heart Gemini, and joint bank accounts would be a good idea unless Cancer is in charge of the finances. Cancer will sprout gray hairs early in life, married to Gemini. If the relationship is kept light, the romantic, unattached couple will have long walks, wonderful talks, and shared interests.

Gemini with Leo

This team makes for interesting conversation. Compatibility is here, for the most part. When brought together, both signs have the tendency to talk about home, family life, and early upbringing. There will be some issues to work on between the two, most notably Leo's desire to talk about themselves all the time and Gemini's need to discuss more worldly matters. Family will be a great source of concern or contentment. If there are stepchildren involved, difficult in-laws and the like, it is important that the two do not draw battlefield lines but work together as a team. When in the courting stages, if Leo is ready to whisper sweet nothings, Gemini needs to stop talking long enough so as not to miss the proposal. Good listening will be one of the key ingredients needed to make this union last.

Gemini with Virgo

I hear a lot of arguing going on in this relationship. In the beginning of such a union, there could be a quick attraction, but as time drags on, these two seem to disagree about everything. These are two very intelligent people for the most part, but put them together and you wouldn't believe the jabs. There is an irritating quality to their relationship. They don't like to be around one another for very long, but they can't stand being apart for any length of time, either. Stay clear unless you're absolutely sure it's true love.

Gemini with Libra

The pairing of these two air signs suggests a long-term commitment. There is something familiar and safe when Gemini and Libra come together. Gemini will find the Libra's intellect stimulating, as well as their physical attributes. They can be best buddies as well as marriage partners. These two could enjoy the same hobbies, music, and sports. Children will play an important role in their lives if they choose to have a family. The major threat of separation could come during the midlife crisis of one of the partners. Therefore, it is of utmost importance that ideals and expectations of the marriage are openly discussed, as often as needed, to avoid breakups.

Gemini with Scorpio

I'm not so sure Gemini could handle Scorpio's strong need for isolation. Scorpios hold much of their thoughts and desires deep within. They communicate through sex. Gemini's constant need for mental stimulation finds no outlet here. Scorpio will be entertained by the Twins but not find the depth they are seeking in this particular sun sign. Jealousy and restrictions could lead to the downfall of this coupling. This combination is great for friends and perhaps working buddies, but for a serious, long-term commitment, save yourself the time and heartache.

Gemini with Sagittarius

Here is a case where opposites attract. For the most part, this could be a lively, healthy, and prosperous pairing. Both signs love travel and change. Sag can talk about religions and philosophies, and Gemini will find these chats interesting. They will show each other a different viewpoint and an opposite way of looking at the world. However, both can be fickle in love. They'll flirt with everyone at a party, although at least they'll leave together. Life's bigger picture is emphasized here, and the attraction is usually mutual. Even though both of these signs possess a wandering eye, the settled Gemini and Sag instinctively seem to know they're not going to stray too far from home.

Gemini with Capricorn

Simply stated, this combination is the young versus the old. Capricorn is the old sign of the zodiac. They live by the rules and relate well to tradition. Gemini is the child in this relationship, breaking all the rules and a few hearts along the way! They can learn from one another. Capricorn can learn to get in touch with their inner child, to enjoy the silly things in life, to take the time to reflect. Gemini can learn discipline, duty, responsibility, and honor. But watch out, Capricorn, because the Gemini will likely break free and wreak havoc in your finely structured life, turning the elite world you've built for yourself upside down. I have seen many affairs between these two signs, chiefly because each sign has what the other lacks. But marriage will seem like a uphill battle. At the least, it will be a scenario of one step forward, three steps back.

Gemini with Aquarius

These two air signs are a solid combination. There could be many happy times. Each goes with the flow and is ready to experience the changes and challenges that life has to offer. They will strive to make theirs the perfect relationship, different from any kind they've toyed with before. They can succeed. The Twins and Water Bearer know communication is very important and work to make sure each other's needs are fulfilled. Gemini will adore Aquarius' quirkiness and marvel at their sense of humor. Aquarius will strive to make sure Gemini is following their highest spiritual path.

Gemini with Pisces

If these two decide to marry, it is likely that escapism will come into play at some point down the road. There will be a denial of truth in the marriage. Communications will be strained, and hurt feelings and misunderstandings will arise. The Pisces personality could drown their sorrows with food, drink, or work. They eventually turn away emotionally. Gemini could live a separate life outside of the marriage. There is often a feeling of never truly being married when these two signs join hands. In good Gemini/Pisces combinations, we usually see the love of family keeping the home fires burning.

Gemini with Aries

Gemini loves the way Aries entices them. They both will enjoy expanding their minds and learning new things together. Aries plays the role of the teacher well, and is more than happy to do so. It is important to note that both signs can be into mind games, so honesty and integrity should not be taken lightly in this particular relationship. There has to be physical attraction between these two, coupled with a sense of humor, to make this union long-lasting. It's a safer bet than most, but caution needs to be exercised in expressing differences of opinion. Otherwise, a simple question over what to have for dinner could lead to all-out war! The overall picture looks bright and promising. Much success is predicted when they work together on a meeting of the minds.

Gemini with Taurus

This is not the best combination for a successful relationship, but I have seen it work more times than not in my practice. I feel the key to these long-lasting unions must be the Taurus' patience with the Gemini, and the acceptance of what each sign needs. As long as Gemini is willing to play the games the Taurus wants to play, things will go well. Gemini can teach the Bull how to have fun! But if Taurus can't get past Gemini's spending habits, unstructured lifestyle, and constant need for variety and change, they will eventually break ties. The success of this commitment comes down to acceptance. It can be trying and difficult in the early years of marriage but has a long-lasting quality as time goes on.

♋

Cancer: The Crab
(June 22–July 22)

Cancer with Cancer

Home and family will be the focus if these two decide to nest. There could be in-law problems. There is mutual understanding and the same security needs. Children will be a necessity in this marriage. One partner can lift and nurture the other's spirit through crises. Cancer men make their women feel safe and protected. Cancer women baby and pamper their men. If trust is ever broken, though, through extramarital affairs, it is likely this union will not survive. Even if they agree to forgive, Cancers never forget.

Cancer with Leo

This relationship mixes fire and water. Though this combination lacks in some areas, there can be a magnetic draw between the two signs. If Cancer can handle Leo's need to be the king or queen of the castle, things will go fine. If the throne is threatened, Leo can become overbearing and insulting, thus hurting Cancer's fragile feelings. The key is for the Crab to allow the Lion to "think" they are in charge, all the time calling their own shots behind the scenes. Leo's heart of gold will touch Cancer deeply, but if the Crab refuses to keep the ego-stroking up, there will be problems. If children take up all of Cancer's attention and energy, the Leo will feel set aside, and that just won't do! There are needs and ego issues that will have to be dealt with in this combo.

Cancer with Virgo

Water and earth signs work well together. Cancer will appreciate the little things the Virgo does around the house. They both know how to squeeze a dollar out of a dime, and both are the best shoppers of all the zodiac signs. Bargains seem to drop into their laps. Cancer, however, will not appreciate Virgo's criticism, especially if it has to do with their mother, their cooking, or their weight. Virgos like to help. They feel that by suggesting improvements, they are helping their mates. Virgo should compliment the Crab and make them feel secure. In turn, Cancer will dedicate themselves to bringing pleasure to the Virgo's everyday world.

Cancer with Libra

This combination is the homebody versus the socialite. Cancer will likely be left crying on the couch while Libra is out on the town in this match. Being with a Crab means you must give constant support, but Libra is busy trying to strike a balance in their own lives. There is much physical attraction in the beginning stages of this type of love, but eventually the same old routine will take over. The same scenes will be played out. Cool Libra will not understand Cancer's emotional mood swings. Libra will work at keeping peace and harmony, but Cancer will want to stir things up, cry a little, and perhaps pout. All they want is attention and to know they are loved! Libras will be looking for the closest exit sign. This pair is better as friends than lovers.

Cancer with Scorpio

The intense emotional nature of these two water signs blends easily. They may not consider one another moody or irrational, as others have suggested they are. However, the Crab and the Scorpion are both master manipulators, though they manipulate in different ways. If defeated, the Crab will back up and side-step, and move from a different angle to get their way. Scorpio usually wins by seducing or hypnotizing you with their eyes or sharp intellect. As long as these two are working on the same goals and there is strong mutual trust, great things can manifest in such a relationship. Both are very psychic, but Scorpios need to show their feelings more when dealing with a Cancer. They need to take the communication farther than just the bedroom for the Cancer to be completely satisfied.

Cancer with Sagittarius

Short term, this duo is a great combination, but long-term commitments prove to be challenging, heartbreaking, and, at the very least, confusing. The fiery sign of Sag wants freedom. These are the Don Juans of the zodiac. The Sag woman is more patient than the Archer man, but that makes no difference when you pair them with a Crab. Sagittarius is trying to escape everything Cancer stands for: home, security, sameness. Sag may enjoy this treat for a while, but then it's back to exploring what's out there in the world (and this means other relationships, too). Cancer will never understand the need for Sag to roam. Sag just hates feeling smothered. The two signs also look at love and sex in very different ways. Sagittarius people are into truth. They tell it like it is. And that may be too much truth for the Cancer to bear. This match produces exciting short-term love affairs, for there is immense attraction. But when the Cancer gets stars in their eyes, things will go downhill fast!

Cancer with Capricorn

Sometimes this combination works. Much depends on how deep the emotional needs of the Cancer are. Capricorns are very stoic. They are logical and direct. Many cannot understand their own feelings much less their partner's. They don't concentrate on abstract things. If the Cappy is too cold and rigid, the Cancer will eventually look for emotional fulfillment elsewhere. What the Goat lacks in emotional ability, they make up for in the financial arena. This could prove to be a money-making couple, especially in the later years. Sexual attraction is very strong between these two. More than likely, the natives will miss one another desperately when they are apart and irritate each other when they are together. However, the relationship does have lasting potential.

Cancer with Aquarius

Aquarius is one of the worst, if not the worst, sign for Cancer to be associated with. Aquarius crave change more than any other sign.

Their cool, aloof nature clashes with the homey, deep feelings Cancer possesses. Many Aquarius do not find much use for the family they were born into. They can check in once or twice a year. Friends and acquaintances enrich their lives. The Cancer cannot cope with or understand these unusual ties. Aquarius do not have time to make small talk about hurt feelings. They have a mission! They want to touch the entire world and make it a better place in which to live. In fact, their mission in life becomes more important than their partner. That's because Aquarius' spiritual path is to help humanity as a whole. But if they fail to keep the home fires burning with their Cancer, it will eventually be put out.

Cancer with Pisces

I have found that if the man in this relationship combo is strong and secure, there will be much success and happiness. If weak, there will be problems with negativity, moodiness, and possible escapism (such as alcohol or drugs). Usually the Crab and the Fish do just fine together. They both are sensitive, psychic beings. Romance plays a big part in the initial courtship. There is mutual satisfaction, trust, and the ability to communicate their feelings without fear of rejection. The research I have done also shows there are more millionaires born under the sign of Pisces than any other sign in the zodiac—and more self-made millionaires born under the sign of Cancer. So this couple could see their dreams come true in a big way!

Cancer with Aries

Sexual attraction is strong here. This relationship allows the couple to experience love on the fast track. But it's a big gamble. Long-term relationships tend to fizzle out, leaving Cancer feeling empty and rejected. While Cancer is still mulling over what went wrong, Aries is already out flirting about town, ready for the next conquest. To Aries, the excitement in a relationship is the chase. For Cancer, it's the capture. Cancer wants to build a secure foundation, but Aries could feel fenced in or bored. This combination could work if the two work a family business together; otherwise, they are both living in their own world.

Cancer with Taurus

Cancer and Taurus fit together like a comfortable pair of jeans and a cozy old sweater. The relationship grows better with time. Cancer's security and financial needs get met, and Taurus' hearty appetite is met in the dining room as well as the bedroom. This can be a long-lasting union, but their closets will be bursting. These two don't discard anything. Clothing, antiques, photos, newspapers—anything that has a purpose is salvaged and saved. That's the way the Crab and the Bull feel about their relationship, too. If it's worth saving, they'll stick together through the hard times and grow stronger in the process.

Cancer with Gemini

If these two signs play together, they can stay together. But more often than not, Cancer assumes the role of the domineering, overly protective parent of the Gemini. Then the relationship becomes one-sided. If these two can work on things as a team, there will be smoother sailing. Gemini will help the Cancer loosen up and play. Cancer will show Gemini they have found someone to trust, to feel safe to be their "twin selves" with. And most of all, Cancers will listen. Talkative Gemini will appreciate the fact that someone is listening sincerely and maybe even taking notes. They will know they are being heard, because Cancer, with their famous memory, will point out declarations of love from years past and, unfortunately, recall the arguments, too. For these two, love doesn't always last, but the friendship certainly can.

♌

Leo: The Lion
(July 23–August 24)

Leo with Leo

This will be a dramatic relationship. The biggest challenge is to decide who will be the Royal Highness. Will they agree to share the
spotlight, or fight for it? There will be much love and admiration,
and these two will make an engaging, attractive couple. It will be
no problem choosing birthday gifts. Anything big, shiny, or gold
will do! Problems could arise if one partner is not supportive of the
other's career goals. This union is sure to include temper tantrums,
but heavy doses of laughter and good times, too.

Leo with Virgo

Since Virgos like to be of service and need to be needed, a match-
up with the majestic Leo sometimes works well. Leo rules, and
Virgo obeys. As long as this cycle remains intact, things will run
smoothly. If Virgo rebels and tries to overpower the throne, there is
likely to be a royal uproar. Note to Leo: Virgos who feel like ser-
vants don't serve as well as those who feel appreciated. Note to
Virgo: Picky Virgos who criticize and make jokes at Leo's expense
will find their services no longer needed.

Leo with Libra

There is potential with this pair. Libras are beautiful people, and
Leo likes a showpiece. Leo will also appreciate Libra's peacekeep-
ing ways. Libra will allow Leo to lead and be happy to follow.
There's one catch, though. Libra expects to be generously rewarded
for what they have to offer. The finer things in life that Leo can so
amply provide are important. Plus, with Leo working day and
night to keep up with the payments, Libra has plenty of time to socialize and enjoy the little extras. Both signs are romantic and giving. They will enjoy shopping together and finding other creative
ways to spend their money.

Leo with Scorpio

The handwriting is on the wall before this relationship even gets off the ground: Run! Run fast! Don't look back! But if you've already decided to try this combination out for yourself, expect major control issues. Keep a box of tissues nearby or, better yet, a suit of armor. These fixed signs seldom find what they're looking for in one another. The sexual arena will be hot for a while, but Scorpio will not allow anyone to truly conquer them. The Leo will deal with their frustrations ferociously for a while, and then probably just give up.

Leo with Sagittarius

Of the three fire signs (Aries, Leo, and Sagittarius), the Archer works the best with Leo. Sag draws energy from the two other fire signs. While Aries rules the head and Leo rules the heart, Sag combines the head and the heart. You won't find the power struggles between Sag and Leo like you will between the Lion and the Ram. Sagittarius will contribute to Leo's positive and enthusiastic outlook on life rather than compete with it. The two will love to travel to foreign places and enjoy lively conversation, and can settle comfortably into a long-term commitment. Part of this is so because Sag doesn't take Leo's commands too seriously. These two can expand each other's world in many favorable ways.

Leo with Capricorn

Capricorn does not have a place in their structured, traditional life for a flashy, overbearing ego, which is how the Goat may view the Lion at first glance. First dates between these two signs usually go nowhere and often end early. If a second date is even considered, Capricorn may catch a glimpse of Leo's strong work ethic and hard-driven spirit. I still conclude that these two would make better business partners than anything else. They both agree that career and social status are important. They just don't relate to one another very well outside of that. Coming from two different perspectives, they could learn much from spending time in one another's world, but the initial attraction would likely fade.

Leo with Aquarius

While Leo is all about "me," Aquarius is about "we," as in "we are the world." Aquarius could get Leo to stretch a little beyond the comfortable little inner circle that the Leo feels so safe in, and that support will make the Lion grateful. Working together toward a common goal will keep Aquarius happy. Social clubs, fundraisers, and mutual friends are all important to keep this relationship ticking. If Leo curbs the tendency to roar out orders, Aquarius will stick around. Both sides enjoy experiencing new things, and this relationship will work well as long as both people are open to moving, updating their education, self-improvement, and keeping up with the times.

Leo with Pisces

Most fire/water sign combinations don't work too well, but I find that this one does more often than not. Pisces love to please. Sometimes they smother. Leos love to be pleased. There is no such thing as too much adoration for the Lion. Therefore, as long as the Pisces doesn't fall into one of their famous "pity parties" and accept the role of the martyr, this combination could prove worthy, despite what most astrology books suggest. Both signs are creative and romantic to the core, and enjoy sharing fantasies. It is worth mentioning that Leo needs to be extrasensitive to Pisces' emotional nature.

Leo with Aries

A no-compete clause needs to be included in the marriage contract between these two. Other than that, things can work out fine. Both have the fire and excitement to excel in life. If Leo will allow Aries the floor every now and then, things will flow more smoothly. These overachievers can amass nice fortunes and reputations. They can build a beautiful life for themselves, but both need to slow down long enough to enjoy it! Sex and romance will be a high-energy experience between these two fiery signs. As long as they put one another first in life, this union can last. Leo needs to sit atop the throne, and Aries high on their pedestal.

Leo with Taurus

Leo could easily get stuck in Taurus' rut, experiencing the same old patterns and situations on a daily basis. This sameness makes the Bull feel secure and content, but Leo the Lion needs to live! Leo cannot force Taurus to do anything. Even a gentle nudge will be met with a defiant stomp of the Bull's hoof. So why fight? Better to find someone else who lives to catch that brass ring. Taurus can offer Leo security and loyalty, but Leo needs more. These two signs seldom see eye to eye.

Leo with Gemini

The Twins add a spark to the Lion's world. They offer many things to Leo in a working and romantic relationship. Geminis have a way with words. They instinctively know what to say and when to say it. Leo loves the praise and flattery that Gemini showers them with. Gemini, in turn, reaps the rewards of Leo's big heart. Since air fans the fire, Gemini will help promote or sell Leo's ideas to the world. Gemini will help keep Leo's spirits up in times of crisis or despair. This is a wonderful combination because it provides each sign with the ability to use their natural gifts: Gemini (communication), Leo (generosity). Travel, friends, and the social scene are all important elements that both signs can enthusiastically share in their relationship.

Leo with Cancer

The issue of who's in charge will likely come up at some point in this relationship. The home is the Leo's castle. The Cancer makes the house a home. Leo needs to relinquish their authority to Cancer in matters regarding the hearth and home, which may not be easy to do. Leos generally ride the fast track in the career world. Because of this, the issue of relocation almost always comes up. It could be deadly to this union if Cancer refuses to move (Cancers seldom move away from the city in which they were born or raised). Sometimes this combination works, usually when both partners are involved in careers. The best bet for making this union last is to own a family business. Both signs are financially savvy. Cancer is the premier promoter, and Leo is the hardest worker. This could lead to a successful partnership in more ways than one.

♍

Virgo: The Virgin
(August 24–September 23)

Virgo with Virgo

Ho hum—too much of the same. This relationship could grow quite dull. It could feel like living with your brother or sister rather than your lover. In this type of relationship, leading a life outside of the union is highly favorable for survival. One must have a fulfilling career, friends, and social activities to avoid that trapped or tied-down feeling. There is not much excitement in the home, although together they could analyze things for hours—and you know the canned goods in the cupboard would be in perfect order!

Virgo with Libra

The Virgo's impeccable taste can help dress the Libra for all of their grand social events. Libra will gently push the reserved Virgo out into that lively social scene. The two can learn much from one another if they are willing to step into each other's world. This is not a match made in heaven, but sometimes it works when the partners accept each other for who they really are. Communication between the two is usually favorable, as Libras intellectualize while Virgos analyze. They both enjoy good gossip, too! Virgo will keep things running smoothly in the household while Libra plans the vacations and dinner parties. The important thing to remember here is to strike a balance between play and work.

Virgo with Scorpio

Scorpio's hypnotic eyes will first attract Virgo, but it's their intriguing mind that keeps the Virgin interested. Scorpio will help Virgo loosen up in the bedroom, too, shedding sexual inhibitions and introducing Virgo to a more intense, passionate type of love. When Scorpio goes into their quiet, moody mode, Virgo may upset the apple cart by analyzing their condition and assuming something is wrong. Let Scorpio alone for a while, Virgo. Give them the space and isolation they so desperately need. Scorpio naturally knows how to "tune you out," so keep the nagging to a minimum. Learn when to step back, Virgo, and this relationship could last a lifetime.

Virgo with Sagittarius

You won't find this relationship combination in the majority, and for good reason. It just doesn't work well. Virgo takes action in precise ways. Sagittarius throws caution to the wind and lives on faith. This couple may never see eye to eye. They may not even be able to live under the same roof. Virgos keep their homes clean, tidy, and in impeccable order. The Sagittarius residence resembles the morning after an all-night party. While Sag is living in the moment, Virgo is steps ahead, planning for the future. This will scare the freedom-loving Sag, who makes no permanent commitments of any kind. However, there could be interesting debates between the two. Unfortunately, they usually turn into arguments, with the Sag bolting for the nearest exit.

Virgo with Capricorn

These two signs are easily drawn to one another. Virgo's down-to-earth approach to life and Capricorn's cautious nature are in harmony. Simple pleasures are enjoyed, and both know the value of a dollar. Home, family, and traditions will play big roles in this partnership. Virgo will teach Capricorn how to loosen up and relax. There will be mutual respect and shared interests. Quiet evenings and weekends at home will be favored over crowded social events. Capricorn will appreciate Virgo's thriftiness and bargain-hunting ability. They can depend on each other. Outsiders may see this relationship as dull and boring, but to the Capricorn and the Virgo, it's comfortable and safe, just the way they like it.

Virgo with Aquarius

Just when Virgo thinks things are settling down in this relationship and there's been a meeting of the minds, Aquarius is demanding changes and wants to try new things. Aquarius, no matter what age, are always in a state of midlife crisis. Both partners are intelligent people, and communication can be a strong point. Virgo needs to settle in one place, however, to build their perfect little world. Aquarius wants to take on the entire universe. Virgo cannot be supportive of Aquarius' constant need for change and challenge. Settling down is what Virgos do best, but Aquarius will never settle. They are always veering off the beaten path, open to new developments and technology. Too many changes, relocations, and abrupt career moves may cause major stress between these two.

Virgo with Pisces

This combination lends itself well to romance. Yet Virgo and Pisces strike a nice balance between romantic love and everyday responsibilities. Both signs play the role of martyr very well. It's important to realize that no one really needs to be saved. Too much smothering and mothering is not good. Individual growth is a must to keep the relationship alive. Often Virgo becomes Pisces' therapist and later resents Pisces if they do not follow the advice given. Pisces could also become too dependent on Virgo for basic needs. The less baggage these signs bring into the relationship, the easier it is.

Virgo with Aries

Since Virgos are apt to think first and act later, they often do not appreciate Aries' "throw caution to the wind" attitude. Aries is a fire sign. They just act upon their natural impulses and pay the consequences later. Aries do not have time or patience to wait around for Virgo to analyze all the little idiosyncrasies of life. Initially, these two could be drawn together because of their brilliant minds, but the long haul is going to be tedious for both signs. A good choice for this combination would be Aries in the role of the supervisor or boss and Virgo as the dutiful worker.

Virgo with Taurus

Taurus will respect Virgo and appreciate the little things they do. Virgo will delight in having a partner on the same wavelength.

These two could spend many happy years together. There is mutual understanding of how life works. But Virgo may anger Taurus if they nag too much about the Bull's diet and weight. Taurus enjoys food! Most Bulls have to be very careful about acquiring the middle-age spread. Virgos are into healthy eating, but Taurus will resist any push or even a gentle nudge away from the dinner table. These two earth signs do have the ability to forge a deep solid bond and are considered one of the more compatible connections in the zodiac.

Virgo with Gemini

Both of these signs have a quick wit and pleasing personality. They will find plenty to talk about and share a sense of humor. This combo works great for friendships, but for love, something seems to be missing. There is an undercurrent in the relationship that something is not right. Day to day, things will not flow smoothly. There is always an issue, a crisis, or something that needs to be dealt with. Virgo may feel like everything rests on their shoulders, taking responsibility for all that is wrong in the relationship. Often Virgo and Gemini use different approaches to achieve the same goals. Just be friends, Virgo. Life will be much easier that way.

Virgo with Cancer

If Virgo can learn to curb their helpful criticism and tiptoe around sensitive Cancer's emotions, things can work out wonderfully. Together, these two can build a dream home, complete with the love and security they both will work hard for. There is a protective quality to this commitment. Each will look after the other, fussing as they go. If Cancer falls into one of their famous moods and clams up, Virgo can draw the Crab out of their shell with a sense of humor. If Virgo is in crisis, Cancer offers a strong shoulder to lean on. This relationship grows even better with time.

Virgo with Leo

There could be instant attraction between these two, but it seldom lasts. Virgo will grow tired of Leo's boastful ways. Leo will expect Virgo to follow, serve, and take orders. Virgo doesn't mind fulfilling this role but needs to feel appreciated for their efforts. Leo can be too flashy and disorganized for the reserved Virgo. Leo will always be at the height of fashion, though, if they let Virgo dress them. Virgo can help organize Leo's busy life, but often there is no time left for the relationship itself. As long as Virgo agrees to play the role of the loyal and dependable worker, the relationship can work. Once Virgo gives their two-week notice, it's over for good.

♎︎

Libra: The Scales
(September 24–October 23)

Libra with Libra

The honeymoon never ends! These two make a beautiful couple. However, there's a strong inclination to party or socialize too much, which could lead to financial problems. Harmony in the home life is strong. This duo will be the envy of family and friends. Often this couple chooses not to have children, content with just the marriage. If they have a family, it is usually not a large one. The focus is strictly on the couple's relationship. They identify with one another. These two believe strongly in the theory of soul mates.

Libra with Scorpio

Libra will be drawn to Scorpio almost immediately. This sign will find Scorpio a wonderful lover but eventually feel overwhelmed by their jealous and possessive personality. Scorpio will demand that Libra cut their many social ties. Libras will find themselves constantly bending to keep the peace. They will walk on eggshells so as not to upset the brooding Scorpio, thus setting bad patterns in the union. When Libras have been pushed to their limit, they will finally stand up for themselves. When all else fails, they will leave. This relationship works short term on a purely sexual level, though long term it's not likely to last.

Libra with Sagittarius

Libra is looking for a commitment. Sagittarius is looking for something a little less permanent. This combination still holds promise. If the Sag is settled, mature, and ready to put down roots, then Libra is a good choice for marriage. If not, Sag will wine and dine the Libra but ultimately disappoint. Size up the Sagittarius before you proceed, dear Libra. That way you won't be setting yourself up for a fall. These two could enjoy just being together. The two movie buffs could have a lot in common. This match makes for a great friendship, too!

Libra with Capricorn

This sometimes works. I am more inclined to advise clients to look to other combinations for a more satisfying relationship. Libra is likely to find Capricorn boring. Libra will enjoy the financial rewards of being with the Goat, but the lovemaking may not be as passionate as they would like. Libra needs romance. Capricorn is very logical when it comes to matters of the heart. The Libra wife cries, "You don't love me!" The Capricorn husband replies, "I pay the mortgage, the car insurance, and the electricity bill. That proves I love you!" Capricorn is too busy with work to indulge in the vacations and parties Libra enjoys. They usually don't grow together, but mostly apart.

Libra with Aquarius

Here are two highly intellectual people. This couple can understand the need for change, and are open to it. Sometimes Aquarius can be a little too cool and aloof for Libra's romantic side. The Water Bearer is not one to whisper sweet nothings, but Libra can help draw their deeply buried sensitive side to the surface. There will always be something to talk about between these two. Plans for the future are discussed early on in the relationship. It's as if they both know they've found the right one.

Libra with Pisces

Romantic love can be found here, but long-term compatibility is another story. Libra adores the dreamy Pisces. The affair seems like a romance novel filled with Pisces' flowery words and kisses. But when the last chapter is read, reality sets in. Libra hangs on, trying to recapture what once was. Pisces gets too comfortable, and the Piscean pity parties start. They whine about everything! It could prove too much for the peace-loving Libra to bear. This couple can dream big beautiful dreams together, but seldom do they live them.

Libra with Aries

Libra is willing to let Aries lead. That's one of the main reasons this match has staying power. These two genuinely like each other. Libra doesn't fuss about Aries flirting with everyone in town because they are too busy doing the same thing. It's usually harmless fun. When dating, Libra feels emotionally needy toward the Aries. Upon marriage, they become strong, self-reliant, confident mates. Libra is the one sign that can twist even the strongest Aries around their little finger. That's because Libras have a tendency to put their partner on a pedestal, and Aries believes they belong there. Libra's undying devotion gives Aries the reassurance they need that they are truly special. Aries, in turn, showers Libra with their own brand of love and affection. Doesn't everyone need to feel special?

Libra with Taurus

Both ruled by the planet Venus, Libra and Taurus will enjoy many of the same luxuries in life: fine art, music, wine, food, and a lavish home. Taurus, however, will not approve of the way shopaholic Libra spends money, and Libra will feel Taurus is a tightwad. It's Wednesday evening. Taurus wants a quiet, early dinner at home. Libra wants to go dancing until the wee hours of the morning. They have some of the same likes, but their personality types may clash. Taurus will be jealous of the time Libra spends with friends. The possessive Taurean nature may be too much for Libra to handle. At some point Libra will ask, "What is more important—financial security or personal freedom?"

Libra with Gemini

The creative natures of the Libra and Gemini bring sexual and intellectual stimulation to this relationship. These folks work together well in business and in love because they know how to communicate. Both love to have fun! They can be kids at heart and often look younger than their age reveals. There is a possible warning for Libra. Geminis are great used-car salesmen. Since Libras are prone to attracting con artists and manipulators, they need to exercise caution! Do not judge a book by its cover. This is not to say that Geminis can't be trusted. Just dig a little deeper, Libra, before you wear your heart on your sleeve. Once you feel comfortable and safe, this relationship can rise to great heights. This could be the very relationship you've been waiting for!

Libra with Cancer

I am amazed at how many marriages I see with this sign combination. The Libra complains a lot about the Cancer's moodiness, and the Cancer feels the Libra is being unsupportive. The sexual attraction that first brought these two together will likely wane. Children will keep the union together longer, but don't count on a fiftieth wedding anniversary. It's best to address issues in this relationship as they come up, rather than letting them smolder beneath the surface. Big blow-ups leave Libra running to cry on their friend's shoulder and Cancer the Crab retreating into their shell for weeks.

Libra with Leo

This combination works better if the man is the Leo. If the Libra lady is appropriately taken care of by her Leo mate, the relationship can be "all that." Libra appreciates the finer things in life. Leo's generous spirit and great financial opportunities could provide the Libra with a life in the lap of luxury. Libra, in turn, will make the Lion feel like the true king he is. There will be parties, mutual friends, exotic vacations, and passionate lovemaking. If the Libra is the male partner in this scenario, he may often feel he is living in the Leo's grander shadow. The Leo woman will be generous but may prefer a more aggressive partner.

Libra with Virgo

Strong family and friendship ties usually last between these two signs, but love and marriage are unlikely unless they serve a financial purpose. Libra's indecisive nature will drive Virgo up the wall. Time is valuable to Virgos and should not be wasted. Yet Virgo will listen contentedly to Libra talk hour after hour about how their day went.

These two signs have great minds, but they may have different values. Libras will look at the big picture and not sweat the small stuff. Virgos, on the other hand, will scrutinize every detail. They must have all the angles covered before they step out into traffic. This could be a very frustrating and time-consuming relationship.

♏

Scorpio: The Scorpion
(October 23–November 22)

Scorpio is the most intense sign in the zodiac. A relationship with a Scorpio will change your life forever. These folks are a force to be reckoned with.

Scorpio with Scorpio

These two have the ultimate sex life! There is great financial power with this couple. There will be control issues to contend with and some knock 'em down, drag 'em out fights. Let's hope these two don't use voodoo dolls when they're angry! Money and sex will keep this relationship going through the hard times. The good times will be filled with their children, special private moments, traveling, acquiring property, and career advancements.

Scorpio with Sagittarius

A sexy fling may be all that comes of this match-up. Sag wants freedom, while Scorpio wants to possess. The first few dates will be great, but the momentum will eventually dwindle. This is not a relationship Sagittarius could easily pop in and out of, like they do with other signs. Scorpio wants all or nothing. You've been properly warned, Sag!

Scorpio with Capricorn

Sexual attraction is strong between these two. Scorpio feels safe with Capricorn. They will argue because Capricorn holds very strong opinions on all subject matters. It is hard for Capricorn to imagine that anyone could hold a differing opinion. Surprisingly, these two can kiss and make up after an argument more quickly than any of the other signs. They can communicate well, and the financial picture should be a bright one. This has all of the makings of a long-term relationship.

Scorpio with Aquarius

Scorpio is too smart to pursue Aquarius. They would irritate one another. There would be constant bickering. Aquarius is not into mind games or submission. The only way for this type of relationship to work is for both partners to take separate vacations, work long hours, and claim different residences (preferably on opposite sides of the country). This is one of the more difficult matches, and I would avoid even thinking of going down that road.

Scorpio with Pisces

These two water signs complement each other. Pisces will be very helpful and caring toward the Scorpio. Pisces natives are like sponges. They tend to soak up other people's problems and feelings. This is not good because Pisces could easily take on the Scorpio's woes. Pisces also smother their loved ones. Scorpios have a deep need for intervals of isolation, and they could resent Pisces crowding their space. If the Pisces is a strong personality, this pair could weave magic into their everyday lives. If Pisces is weak, they will be left feeling alone most of the time.

Scorpio with Aries

Most Scorpios don't find Aries to their liking. They can see through Aries' little mind games and power plays right away. At times, sexual sparks fly, but by the time they dance around one another, nothing gets off the ground. Jealous Scorpio will not stand for Aries flirting with others. The time and energy spent on trying to make this relationship work is probably not worth the end result. Infidelity, money, and control issues will come up again and again.

Manipulation tactics will likely be used by each sign to gain the upper hand. Trust, or the lack of it, will be a big problem.

Scorpio with Taurus

"I've met my match!" cries the delighted Scorpio. Taurus' sexual drive is almost as strong as Scorpio's. These two hardheaded, jealous, possessive signs will bring out the best in one another. They expect the same things from their mate: loyalty, devotion, and fidelity. They will succeed in attaining great financial fortune if they work together. Both will probably keep secret bank accounts in their own names because of their controlling nature, but joint resources will grow over the years, giving the couple the security they so desire. These two have bad tempers but express them quite differently. The Taurus temper builds up and erupts like a massive volcano. Then it simmers back down. Scorpio will be more secretive, plotting out their revenge with a smile upon their face. If this couple can learn to not take the little arguments so seriously, this relationship could last a lifetime.

Scorpio with Cancer

These two emotional, psychic signs know just the right thing to say or do to lift each other's spirits. If they are both depressed at the same time, we have quite a problem! The relationship will be centered around the family and building their own traditions. Scorpio and Cancer have photographic minds. They don't miss anything. It's important that they fight fair and agree to peace treaties. Issues not resolved could come up years later. Both are excellent at manipulating situations to their benefit. They'd run a great family business. Scorpio has to be careful that their stinging criticism doesn't hurt the Crab, while Cancers need to learn not to take things too personally.

Scorpio with Leo

Scorpio can only take so much of the Lion. Many times Scorpions find they just don't like the kind of energy Leo gives out. This relationship will have more than its share of emotional outbursts and power struggles. Royal Leo roars, "I am your king," but Scorpio bows to no one. There's a mixing of fire and water here. Leo may think they are winning this battle, but Scorpio will ultimately win the war, even if it means the death of the relationship.

Scorpio with Virgo

This type of relationship usually starts out as a friendship and develops over time. If it leads to commitment, Scorpio and Virgo will settle down nicely. Arguments are likely to be over little silly things that don't seem so silly at the time. Scorpio will resort to the silent-treatment tactic, and Virgo will try to analyze the situation and determine the root of the problem. The best antidote for a happier marriage between the two is not to sweat the small stuff. Most of the time this combination works great. But Virgo must accept the fact that living with *any* Scorpio is never easy.

Scorpio with Libra

There is mutual admiration and attraction here, but the fireworks won't last. Scorpio would be able to control Libra and eventually realize there is no test or challenge in this relationship. Scorpios are not afraid of confrontation. Libra runs from it. Sometimes when things are running smoothly in a relationship, Scorpio will try to stir the pot a little, just to create some friction. The relationship seems more exciting to them that way. More importantly, they'll get the chance to kiss and make up! Peace-loving Libra won't buy into their little schemes. The relationship will remain stagnant and never grow. Friends? Yes! Lovers? For a little while. Husband and wife? Forget it!

♐

Sagittarius: The Archer
(November 23–December 22)

Sagittarius with Sagittarius

If their brutal honesty doesn't kill the relationship, the two Archers may have a good thing. If the relationship is not working, both have the sense to move on to greener pastures without hesitation and long, drawn-out good-byes. Usually the couple can work through almost any problem because of their positive natures. "Nothing is as bad as it seems" and "things will be better tomorrow" are the mottos Sagittarius live by. Sports, travel, religious pursuits, and gambling are some of the pastimes these couples will enjoy.

Sagittarius with Capricorn

Sagittarius fight to break the very restraints and traditions Capricorns work to build. The two may enjoy each other's company and no-nonsense approach to life, but there is no place for the freedom-loving Sagittarius in Capricorn's organized world. Sag wouldn't want to live there too long anyway. There are too many places to see, people to meet, and hearts to conquer. Capricorn will never understand the Sagittarius wanderlust, but they will secretly envy it. This is not a "till death do we part" kind of love.

Sagittarius with Aquarius

Here we have two freedom and truth seekers who don't mind abrupt changes sweeping them off in new directions. They both hate to be tied down and will try anything once. Sagittarius and Aquarius are a great match! They will talk about spiritual paths and learn to meditate together. Aquarius expects loyalty, so if the Sagittarius is really ready to make that kind of commitment, Aquarius should jump at the chance. Their life together will be one of great exploration!

Sagittarius with Pisces

The negative side of the Pisces is going to hurt the chances of a long-lasting relationship with Sagittarius. The optimistic Archer wants to hear only the happy stories in life and not be burdened with crises. Pisces will feel they're getting no support from Sag during the hard times. Pisces' constant smothering will give Sagittarius justification for leaving the relationship. The two will not see eye to eye on anything. Pisces may not accept reality and try to win the Sagittarius back long after the breakup. These couples are the type that end up on the *Jerry Springer Show*.

Sagittarius with Aries

While some signs may find Aries too aggressive and bold for their taste, Sagittarius adores what Aries can bring to a relationship. The Archer and the Ram find much to gab about. They agree that one should take risks and that nothing is impossible. If they choose to commit, they will find sexual compatibility, and they will share a love for knowledge and higher education. They will allow one another to take turns playing the role of teacher and student. Travel, eating out every other night, and fast cars will be some of their life's pleasures.

Sagittarius with Taurus

That Sagittarius charm draws the Taurus, but there's not much else to hold this relationship together for long. When the Bull's possessive side comes charging out, Sag will have no choice but to run. Sag favors their personal freedom over money, although they'd like to keep both. But if it came right down to it, Sag wouldn't let anyone fence them in. The famous Taurus temper is also something Sagittarius will not tolerate. Money-making ventures would be highly profitable between the two, but I wouldn't gamble a dime on this relationship working out.

Sagittarius with Gemini

The Archer and the Twins take their time getting to the altar. There's no rush to settle down, according to these two. By the time the "I do's" are exchanged, these signs often know exactly what they want in a committed relationship. As long as they both remain faithful to each other, Sagittarius and Gemini could enjoy a blessed union. They would be supportive of one another's goals. The communication lines are always open. The two share many of the same interests and hobbies, and both love to bargain-shop. Besides being lovers, Sag and Gemini could be the best of friends. Go for it!

Sagittarius with Cancer

Their souls connect. Their eyes meet. They are drawn to one another across the crowded room. The Sagittarius/Cancer love affair offers romance-novel writers great material. However, this couple would be better off reading the book than living it. Most of these connections don't end happily ever after. This is very confusing because the initial attraction is so strong: Sag and Cancer are like two magnets. They can't stay away from one another. Eventually, the Crab's need to settle down will suffocate the freedom-loving Archer. Arguments are par for the course. The relationship is on and off for months, even years, until they realize it doesn't meet their individual needs.

Sagittarius with Leo

These two signs love to have fun. They will live for the moment and dream big! This is a relationship that would never get dull. Money-making ventures and business deals prove lucky. However, they both need to be cautious about gambling too much, because the fun could turn into an addiction. There are usually no complaints in the bedroom. Leo will need to curb their bossy tendencies, and Sag needs to be gentle with Leo's ego. The biggest concern is overindulgence. Leo and Sagittarius do nothing halfway. It's usually to the extreme. They believe in living life to the fullest and often on the edge!

Sagittarius with Virgo

Let's look at an ordinary week in the life of Sagittarius and Virgo. There are seven days in the week. The first three days are just wonderful. Things run smoothly. The couple is in love. They laugh. They talk. Then the fourth day hits, and it's all downhill from there. Little arguments start. They pick on each other. They can't stand to be in the same room. The battle lines are drawn. The less time these two spend together, the longer the relationship will last. It's that simple. Too much togetherness will mean the death of this union. Personalities clash and defenses go up. It would be best to avoid this connection.

Sagittarius with Libra

Many times in a Sagittarius/Libra relationship there is what appears to be a permanent breakup. More often than not, this couple gets a second chance. Sag is hard to tie down. They need to get their wanderlust out of their system before they make a lifetime commitment. Libra, on the other hand, has been waiting for the church bells to ring all of their life. These two can enjoy a great relationship, but the timing has to be right. When Sag has explored all of life's curiosities, they will likely come back for Libra. Hopefully, Sagittarius won't make Libra wait too long.

Sagittarius with Scorpio

Crises usually bring couples closer together. In the Sagittarius/ Scorpio relationship, a crisis could pull them apart. This relationship will have more than its share of problems. Each sign deals with problems in different ways. Scorpios want answers immediately. They are intense, emotional personalities. Sagittarius is apt to take a more carefree, lighthearted approach to issues. Thus, Scorpio feels Sagittarius doesn't really care. Issues of jealousy, fidelity, and money will likely come up. There is passion, but the flames may die out if Scorpio's emotional needs don't get met too.

♑

Capricorn: The Goat
(December 23–January 20)

Capricorn with Capricorn

Both career-driven individuals, this couple will have to set aside time to see one another. The great wealth they could accumulate is undeniable, but arguments could arise about how to spend it. The earlier years of the commitment/marriage will be filled with hard work, juggling family and career along with the normal squabbles. In later years, the craziness starts. Capricorns mature earlier then most other signs. Therefore, they miss out on enjoying their teenage and young adult years. After middle age sets in, they realize they want to live the childhood they never had. They can act irrationally. Marriage can feel restricting. It's important at the time that the couple balance their new ideas with the traditions they've established in the past in order for their lives to run smoothly.

Capricorn with Aquarius

The Aquarius New Age ideals will clash with the traditional ways of the Capricorn. Aquarius seeks change and is constantly looking toward the future. Capricorn hangs on tightly to the past and does not easily accept change. This couple's tastes are worlds apart. The Goat favors the Rolex watch, the Gucci suit, and designer glasses. The Water Bearer may sport the latest fads: tattoos, body piercing, and the latest hairdo complete with purple highlights!

Capricorn with Pisces

Pisces will help Capricorn understand and escape into their subconscious. They will open their world to dreams, romance, and fantasy. It may take a little nudging on the part of the Fish, but Capricorn will find the Pisces personality a nice retreat after a hard day at the office. Pisces will help the Capricorn relax and not look at the world too seriously. Capricorn can help bring Pisces back down to earth if they wander too far from reality. Their spirits can intertwine. Generally, this combination works if the couple looks at one another as equals.

Capricorn with Aries

Things move too fast in this relationship for Capricorn. Cappy doesn't approve of Aries' pushy, impractical attitude. Aries doesn't want to wait for anything! Their pioneering spirit forces them to make drastic changes on the spur of the moment. Aries is too much for Capricorn to handle. The cautious Goat needs to sit and think before making a decision, but Aries doesn't have time to sit around. They need to take action! One partner is always a step ahead or a step behind the other.

Capricorn with Taurus

These two earth signs have what it takes to make a relationship work. Their basic needs are the same, and they are actually quite alike. There will be arguments over money. Security-driven Taurus expects to handle all of the finances. Organized Capricorn thinks they're the best person for the job. Separate accounts may be a good idea for these two. Hardworking Capricorn may find Taurus a little lazy when it comes to work around the house. Other than that, the relationship is very comfortable.

Capricorn with Gemini

Since Capricorn represents the mature, responsible, old sign of the zodiac, it does not connect well with Gemini, the youthful, fun-loving sign. They can offer one another a fresh new way of looking at things and a much different opinion. Flexible Gemini will be more than happy to share their ideas. However, Capricorn is very opinionated and may feel Gemini's views are just a waste of their valuable time.

Capricorn with Cancer

Here is a case where opposites attract. Cancer could make the most magnificent home for Capricorn, complete with all of the family traditions and loyalties Capricorn is so attached to. Capricorn can supply Cancer with the financial security they need. The problems arise when logical Capricorn does not take Cancer's supersensitive feelings into consideration. The cold exterior of the Capricorn doesn't melt for many, but Cancer is the one sign that has the capability to soften the old Goat up.

Capricorn with Leo

The Goat and the Lion can be workaholics. They often work long days and take on any extra hours thrown their way. They identify themselves by what they do for a living. How they spend their paychecks is quite a different story. Leo thinks Capricorn is a tightwad with money. Capricorn feels Leo should be put on a restricted allowance so they don't blow it all on Saturday night. There is some truth to both beliefs. Capricorn is happy to spend nights and weekends at their lovely home. Leo enjoys family but likes to be the social butterfly and often is in the spotlight. Leo's flashy style clashes with Capricorn's more reserved demeanor. Anything more than a business partnership may not last.

Capricorn with Virgo

The Capricorn/Virgo relationship works like a charm. Their lives will be organized, orderly, conservative, and a bit boring. This is the couple who will have their mortgage paid off, their kids married, and a great retirement program set up by age fifty. They work together for the same things in life, and communicate on the same wavelength. Virgo's coupon-clipping abilities will be admired by the Capricorn, who believes in saving for rainy days, too. The excitement in this couple's life comes from everything running smoothly.

Capricorn with Libra

Save yourself some time and money, Capricorn, and look elsewhere for love. On the surface, this relationship looks promising. Capricorn and Libra enjoy nice things, designer fashions, and a high social status. But the couple will be at odds over their free time. Their hobbies and interests are different. Social Libra may want to party or dance all night long. Capricorn is early to bed, early to rise. If a balance is not struck between the two, they will go off in different directions.

Capricorn with Scorpio

Capricorn and Scorpio are private people. Reserved, quiet, and sometimes aloof, these two come alive in the bedroom. They enjoy each other's company and will work hard at any problems or crises that comes up in a marriage. Concerns arise when Scorpio's emotional side is neglected by Capricorn. The Goat is very logical in love. Seldom do they bring their partner flowers and candy. Capricorn needs to learn that offering a shoulder to lean on is sometimes better than giving practical advice. Scorpio hears Capricorn say, "I love you," but they need to feel it, too.

Capricorn with Sagittarius

This is not one of the best combinations for love. This relationship will have a short fuse. Since both signs enjoy a good debate, communication presents no problem for this pair, but the physical attraction is not strong. Sagittarius breaks tradition too much for Capricorn to feel safe. Capricorns are always on time for their appointments and dates. They often arrive early. Sagittarius are notoriously late. Their housekeeping habits would drive Capricorn up the wall. Sagittarius doesn't mind clutter. They're known to have messy bachelor pads. Tidy Capricorn has a place for everything. They are known for having clean, organized closets. If these two decide to make a go of it, Capricorn will have to loosen up a little, and Sagittarius will have to buy a watch!

Aquarius: The Water Bearer
(January 21–February 19)

Aquarius with Aquarius

If both are working toward the same goals, this duo can expect great happiness. Think of all the growth and spiritual development they will experience. They both understand the need for change. Life will never be boring. This couple will try the latest foods, hairstyles, and fads. Their home will be full of the latest gadgets and new technology. Pets will be treated like royal members of the family. Friends who drop by to visit could find the hospitality so inviting that they end up staying way past their welcome. Politics, humanitarian efforts, and the internet will be shared interests.

Aquarius with Pisces

If this relationship gets past the first phone call or e-mail, then it has potential. These two signs communicate so differently. Pisces could find Aquarius condescending. Aquarius says Pisces is too shallow. The first date will lay the basis for who's in control of this relationship. If Aquarius takes over, Pisces will feel left out around all of Aquarius' friends. Pisces wants to explore their romantic dreams, and Aquarius is too technical when it comes to the theory of love. If Pisces takes the lead, Aquarius will soon grow bored, tired of the smothering and Pisces' constant need for reassurance. Just be friends.

Aquarius with Aries

Here's a good gamble. Aries are willing to try anything once. They are strong and self-assured and have lots to say. Aquarius will appreciate the positive, upbeat personality of the Ram. When they argue, they will fight fair. Often, there will be no resolution because both signs are the know-it-alls of the zodiac. They can learn a lot from one another if they just listen. This will be one of the few relationships in which Aries will feel like someone is on their side. Aries demand to be number one. With Aquarius, they'll never have to ask for admiration or support, because it'll be right there. In turn, Aries will encourage the Water Bearer to go after their wildest dreams.

Aquarius with Taurus

Disappointment will be no stranger to this relationship. Taurus and Aquarius are fixed signs. They don't bend easily. Taurus will not permit Aquarius to volunteer for every community effort in town. There's dinner to be made, and bills to pay, and the Taurus needs attention. Aquarius needs the energy they draw from other people. They feel alive and connected to the universe when they are with their friends. It's important for Aquarius to know they are contributing to society in some way. Taurus does not relish change, while Aquarius craves it. Sometimes differences in a relationship are healthy, but here they could prove otherwise.

Aquarius with Gemini

The energy between these two air signs flows nicely. They can talk nonsense for hours! If there's serious business to discuss, these quick minds will work together to get the job done. There's not much bickering here. Power struggles are few and far between. Friends are welcome anytime, day or night. This couple also would work well together in the areas of research or teaching. The attraction can last throughout the years because both are willing to pursue new ideas. Although the word "forever" isn't in either sign's vocabulary, Aquarius and Gemini do agree never to say "never."

Aquarius with Cancer

Some astrology books claim this relationship has its potential. In my practice, it has proved to be one of the most difficult to maintain and derive any pleasure from. The differences between the two signs produce attraction in the initial stage of romance. But Aquarius cannot give the moody Cancer the emotional security they need, and home and family-loving Cancer cannot give Aquarius the freedom to make sweeping changes in their lives. Both have completely different purposes to fulfill in this lifetime. Very likely, the things Cancer holds most dear are things the Aquarius usually is not interested in. I have seen major problems between these signs, whether the relationship was that of love, work, or family. Friendships seem to be a different story. Aquarius treat their friends like Cancer would treat their family. Cancer and Aquarius, just be friends!

Aquarius with Leo

Aquarius and Leo are opposing signs but can still find a harmonious balance to make their relationship long-lasting. They are opposites but possess some of the same strong desires and goals. Both have big hearts, but show them off in different ways. The Leo heart will be generous when in love. They will shower the object of their affection with gifts and special attention. The Aquarius heart is big when it comes to helping the world. They give to the homeless, less fortunate, and underprivileged. These two can learn a lot from one another. Leo can learn that the power of love comes back when you give it away. The more people you touch, the more your life will be blessed. Aquarius can learn, through Leo, that sharing begins in the home.

Aquarius with Virgo

Virgo will certainly make Aquarius more aware of their responsibilities in life. Aquarius doesn't care to hear about the mundane things in life, but there are bills to pay! A Virgo woman will have a "honey do" list ready every weekend. Never mind if Aquarius has plans with his buddies. Virgo knows that more important things come first. They will bicker about money and household chores. The Virgo man will not approve of the Aquarius woman's funky fashion statements. He may try to squash her sense of style. Compromise is the only way this relationship can survive.

Aquarius with Libra

The potential for happiness is strong with these lovebirds. Libra won't argue like other signs when Aquarius needs to make drastic lifestyle changes. As long as Libra is part of those changes, all will be fine! The intellectual and creative energies these two possess is a turn-on. Libra can bring balance to Aquarius' erratic life. Friends are like family here, and socializing is a big part of their relationship.

Aquarius with Scorpio

The Aquarius can handle a demanding career, family, and a couple of worthy causes, but it's unlikely they'll be able to handle the Scorpio. Don't even try, Aquarius. The intense Scorpio will not allow you to get your way. There will be no lifestyle changes without their approval. Scorpio will make you pay if you try to do anything sneaky. So why waste your energy?

Aquarius with Sagittarius

What a delightful match! Aquarius and Sagittarius can enrich each other's lives. They have much to share. Both are determined to make the best of whatever it is that life hands them. They are willing to grab the brass ring, and they do it with such passion that it spills over into their relationship. The couple's calendar will be full with busy career activities and plans with friends. If Sagittarius has truly settled down, then expect longevity in this relationship. If not, the romance will be marked by highs and lows but undoubtedly will be a very special one.

Aquarius with Capricorn

Cautious Capricorn prefers the tried and true, while Aquarius wants to try new things. There's a definite clash of ideas when these two get together. Capricorn will not find the steadiness they are looking for in such a relationship. They must learn to expect the unexpected if they pursue this union. Aquarius could feel restricted in the commitment, never finding the freedom they need to be true to themselves.

♓

Pisces: The Fish
(February 20–March 21)

Pisces with Pisces

Pisces people are so indecisive that they frustrate themselves. They find it hard to make decisions because they see both sides of a situation and don't want to feel guilty if they make the wrong choice. If they ever make up their mind to walk down the aisle, what a romantic fairy tale they could tell! The truth is, Pisces live soap-opera lives. There is always a crisis or concern to overcome. The emotional roller coaster ride they would take together may never end! It would be better to settle down with one of the earth signs—Taurus, Capricorn, or Virgo—to help with grounding. But if they're sure they've found their soul mate, Pisces can dream big dreams together and live a life of romantic escape.

Pisces with Aries

Aries may grow tired of Pisces' incessant whining, but they love the attention Pisces showers on them. As long as Pisces doesn't smother, Aries will look down from their pedestal with appreciation. This relationship benefits Aries more than Pisces in the long run, but the two can make a go of it if both parties share the responsibilities of commitment.

Pisces with Taurus

Taurus will need to watch their temper around sensitive Pisces, whose feelings could easily get bruised. But overall, this match works. Taurus need a lot of attention and affection, so Pisces could smother and mother all they want! The Bull will help bring Pisces back down to earth when they are caught up in their dream world. If they can't make a decision, logical Taurus will make it for them. Worries are lifted! Romance, candlelight, fine wine, and true love would last a lifetime for these two.

Pisces with Gemini

A dating relationship of this sort should not be taken too seriously. The Gemini would probably agree, but if Pisces falls head over heels in love, there's danger ahead! Gemini's fickle nature and need for variety will bring Pisces great disappointment. The two could carry on brilliant conversations. Their creative minds work well together. But Pisces won't be able to see through their rose-colored glasses that a long-term commitment will not work. The Fish may hang on to the relationship long after Gemini has moved on.

Pisces with Cancer

This pair would be worth betting on. Pisces and Cancer tend to get depressed more often than most of the other signs. Cancers can get quite moody around the full moon. Pisces are like sponges—they soak up everything in their environment. If the couple's moods are in harmony most of the time, the relationship will work. If there are many emotional ups and downs, there will be problems. Their basic natures are to be caring, sympathetic, and kind. If they bring these qualities out in one another, the union will prosper.

Pisces with Leo

Here's where Pisces can play their role very well. Pisces love to please, and Leos love to be pleased. But it's a two-way street. Leos need to make sure they don't take Pisces for granted, or they'll become a cold fish. Most astrologers say this is not a match made in heaven. I agree, but I have seen many cases that have worked out wonderfully. If there's mutual compassion and both parties benefit, I like the idea.

Pisces with Virgo

These opposites could easily make things work if they take the time to listen more to each other. They actually make a pretty good team. Virgo will fuss over Pisces' health, and Pisces will just fuss. Their home is apt to be filled with children, pets, extended family, and chaos. Virgos like to help people, and Pisces like to please people. This couple could run a successful business working with the public, too. Things won't always run smoothly. These folks tend to bite off more than they can chew, but it's workable.

Pisces with Libra

These two signs both have indecisive minds. They would probably drive each other nuts, but they hate to offend. Pisces likes to stir up the pot every now and then, while Libra hates confrontation. The upside to this union is the romance. But in the long run, the relationship could be frustrating and wear thin.

Pisces with Scorpio

Intense Scorpio may be too much for Pisces to handle over the long haul. The relationship has its merits, though. Pisces indulge Scorpio in their wildest fantasies. Pisces will also find Scorpio to be a strong ally in their corner during times of adversity and crisis. Scorpio's natural healing powers can soothe Pisces' worries and emotional ups and downs. If they are at odds, Scorpio's influence will not be a healthy one for Pisces' emotional well-being.

Pisces with Sagittarius

This is one of those relationship in which gullible, trusting Pisces could get hurt. If the Sagittarius is mature and has truly settled down, then the relationship will be strained at times but can work. If the Sagittarius is still seeking freedom, Pisces are likely setting themselves up for disappointment. Smothering in this type of relationship doesn't work for Pisces—it backfires. Freedom-loving Sag will not appreciate everything they do. This relationship could be very one-sided.

Pisces with Capricorn

The Capricorn could easily take on the role of parent in this relationship, with Pisces, of course, being the child. If this happens, the relationship is doomed. It may last, but each partner will feel unfulfilled. It's best if each has a successful career and separate goals, and interests to bring to the relationship. Mutual respect is a must for survival. This nice blend of a water and an earth sign lends itself to even more compatibility. The two should get along very well. Stoic Capricorn may not always understand Pisces' strong, emotional nature, but it will help soften their heart a little.

Pisces with Aquarius

Go ahead and meet for lunch, but I wouldn't agree to anything more than that. These two make better friends than lovers. They could ruin a wonderful friendship if they step over the line. Aquarius need their space. Pisces may take this as rejection. As a business team, they'd do well. Pisces' creative abilities, coupled with the Aquarius' technical brain, could invent or create a huge money-making venture. But romance is likely to be a letdown.

Final Thoughts

My wish is that you have enjoyed this book! Hopefully it has made you laugh, cry, and ponder your own situations and relationships. Perhaps you've gained some new ideas and insights.

Remember, any time you affirm the positive in your partner, you are affirming the positive in your relationship, and that's what you get back. Thoughts are like boomerangs. Those good qualities you so love and desire in your mate will slowly start to expand. If you fuss, nag, complain, and dwell on the negative qualities, your relationship will become negative as well. Sometimes it seems much more difficult to focus on the positive things in a relationship, and so easy to dwell on the negative. I'm suggesting you raise the spiritual energy in your marriage or commitment. Cherish the fact that you two soul mates even connected in the first place. Some souls never locate their true mate. Most importantly, you should honor your soul-mate connection with love and respect. Don't allow a day to go by where you forget to honor this magical connection and deep love.

The soul-mate type of love can transform your very being. It can make you a better person. On an unconscious level, all human beings know this. That's why everyone is seeking and searching for this unique connection. Honor the spirit that lies within each other, and allow one another to make mistakes. For it is in the trial and error that we grow and learn. You can't have rainbows without rain.

Begin by looking at all of the relationships that enter your life as a gift. Whether they are a positive or negative influence, each person possesses a gift to help you grow spiritually. Chance meetings are not coincidental. The people you work next to at the office have a purpose in your life, some more meaningful than others, but still a divine purpose. Those you choose to be with sexually or romantically have an even more profound purpose.

The next time you meet someone, ask yourself, what am I supposed to learn from this person? Even if you politely strike up a conversation for a few minutes waiting in line at a grocery store, there's something to learn. Maybe someone just flashes you a smile and that brightens your mood. Or perhaps you accept a job under a tyrant boss. Why are you spiritually in this position? What is it that you must learn from this person, either about yourself or the situation?

Each and every one of us is divine. We have a physical sense but also a spiritual sense. Because we can see, hear, and touch others physically, it's easy to look at people only in a physical sense. But take a moment to ponder their spiritual essence. How do you feel about them? Most of the time when we reflect back on past relationships, we understand what our soul's lesson was. The exciting part about meeting someone new is we don't always grasp the lesson. It's a mystery. But we learn as we go. If we take the time to stop and examine our personal relationships every now and then, the picture becomes clearer of why we're really together and what we're here to learn.

I urge you to begin looking at all of your relationships in a spiritual sense, and feel blessed. We all come together for a purpose. We touch others' lives at the same time they bring an awareness to ours. The most meaningful part of life is not financial gain or career strides, it's our relationships with others. There are constant exchanges each and every day. And they may be more meaningful than you've ever imagined!

Much love, Maria

Notes

To Write to the Author

If you wish to contact the author or would like more information about this book, please write to the author in care of Llewellyn Worldwide and we will forward your request. Both the author and publisher appreciate hearing from you and learning of your enjoyment of this book and how it has helped you. Llewellyn Worldwide cannot guarantee that every letter written to the author can be answered, but all will be forwarded. Please write to:

Maria Shaw
℅ Llewellyn Worldwide
P.O. Box 64383, Dept. 0-7387-0746-5
St. Paul, MN 55164-0383, U.S.A.

Please enclose a self-addressed stamped envelope for reply,
or $1.00 to cover costs. If outside U.S.A., enclose
international postal reply coupon.

Many of Llewellyn's authors have websites with additional information and resources. For more information, please visit our website at http://www.llewellyn.com

Free Magazine

Read unique arti-
cles by Llewellyn authors,
recommendations by experts, and information
on new releases. To receive a **free** copy of
Llewellyn's consumer magazine, *New Worlds of
Mind & Spirit,* simply call 1-877-NEW-WRLD or
visit our website at www.llewellyn.com and
click on *New Worlds.*

) LLEWELLYN ORDERING INFORMATION

Order Online:
Visit our website at www.llewellyn.com, select your books, and order
them on our secure server.

Order by Phone:
- Call toll-free within the U.S. at 1-877-NEW-WRLD
  (1-877-639-9753). Call toll-free within Canada at
  1-866-NEW-WRLD (1-866-639-9753)
- We accept VISA, MasterCard, and American Express

Order by Mail:
Send the full price of your order (MN residents add 7% sales tax) in
U.S. funds, plus postage & handling to:

> **Llewellyn Worldwide**
> **P.O. Box 64383, Dept. 0-7387-0746-5**
> **St. Paul, MN 55164-0383, U.S.A.**

Postage & Handling:

Standard (U.S., Mexico, & Canada). If your order is:
$49.99 and under, add $3.00
$50.00 and over, FREE STANDARD SHIPPING

AK, HI, PR: $15.00 for one book plus $1.00 for
each additional book.

International Orders (airmail only):
$16.00 for one book plus $3.00 for each additional book

Orders are processed within 2 business days.
Please allow for normal shipping time. Postage and handling rates subject to change.

Maria Shaw's Book of Love
Horoscopes, Palmistry, Numbers,
Candles, Gemstones & Colors

MARIA SHAW

A love manual exclusively for teens! What should I wear on a first date? Is a Taurus a good match for an Aries? How can I turn a crush into something more? Maria Shaw answers these and other questions in this entertaining love manual, written exclusively for teens.

Young adults will have fun looking up their astrological love match in the comprehensive compatibility guide and calculating their "love number" through numerology. This jam-packed love guide also shows teens how to use simple palmistry, candle magic, colors, gemstones, and crystals for attracting someone special, asking someone out, overcoming jealousy, avoiding a breakup, and other issues of the heart.

0-7387-0545-4, 240 pp., 7½ x 9⅛, illus. $14.95

To order, call 1-877-NEW-WRLD
Prices subject to change without notice

Maria Shaw's Star Gazer

MARIA SHAW

The only comprehensive guide to the New Age written for teens. You've seen Maria Shaw on Fox News, heard her on America Talk Radio. She's been in the national spotlight appearing on television shows from *Blind Date* to *Soap Talk* to the *Anna Nicole Smith Show* (counseling Anna on her personal relationships).

Maria Shaw's Star Gazer helps teens discover who they are through their zodiac signs. It gives a numerology formula to predict the next nine years of life; how-tos for reading palms, the tarot, and auras; guides to crystals, candle magic, and dreams; and techniques for developing intuitive abilities.

0-7387-0422-9, 336 pp., 7½ x 9⅛, illus. $17.95

To order, call 1-877-NEW-WRLD
Prices subject to change without notice

MARIA SHAW'S TAROT KIT FOR TEENS
(Includes Lo Scarabeo Universal Tarot deck)

MARIA SHAW

A fun introduction to the Tarot—exclusively for young adults.

Teens who want to discover and unlock their psychic abilities will find no better guide than Maria Shaw, who has a knack for making new age topics accessible to the young adult market.

Maria covers all the basics, from a smattering of history to in-depth descriptions of all major and minor arcana cards. Common concerns such as how to prepare for a reading, how to cut the cards, how to ask questions, and how to choose the best days for readings are discussed in detail. Sixteen different card spreads, including teen love layouts, the guardian angel/spirit guide spread, and the big question spread, give new readers lots of options. The deck itself is age-appropriate, containing non-threatening images that are appealing to young adult interests.

0-7387-0523-3, Boxed kit (5½ x 8⅝) includes 78 full-color cards, black bag, and 192-pp., illus. guidebook $19.95

Soul Mates
Understanding Relationships Across Time

RICHARD WEBSTER

The eternal question: how do you find your soul mate—that special, magical person with whom you have spent many previous incarnations? Popular metaphysical author Richard Webster explores every aspect of the soul mate phenomenon in his newest release.

The incredible soul mate connection allows you and your partner to progress even further with your souls' growth and development with each incarnation. *Soul Mates* begins by explaining reincarnation, karma, and the soul, and prepares you to attract your soul mate to you. After reading examples of soul mates from the author's own practice, and famous soul mates from history, you will learn how to recall your past lives. In addition, you will gain valuable tips on how to strengthen your relationship so it grows stronger and better as time goes by.

1-56718-789-7, 216 pp., 6 x 9 $12.95

To order, call 1-877-NEW-WRLD
Prices subject to change without notice

Life Between Lives
Hypnotherapy for Spiritual Regression

MICHAEL NEWTON, PH.D.

A famed hypnotherapist's groundbreaking methods of accessing the spiritual realms.

Dr. Michael Newton is world-famous for his spiritual regression techniques that take subjects back to their time in the spirit world. His two bestselling books of client case studies have left thousands of readers eager to discover their own afterlife adventures, their soul companions, their guides, and their purpose in this lifetime.

Now, for the first time in print, Dr. Newton reveals his step-by-step methods. His experiential approach to the spiritual realms sheds light on the age-old questions of who we are, where we came from, and why we are here.

0-7387-0465-2, 240 pp., 6 x 9, illus. $14.95

To order, call 1-877-NEW-WRLD
Prices subject to change without notice

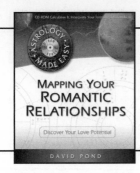

Mapping Your Romantic Relationships

Discover Your Love Potential

DAVID POND

Strengthen your love connection through astrology.

Do you understand your mate? Would you like to improve your relationship with your partner or spouse? One way to gain entry into the mysterious realm of romantic relationships is through astrology.

David Pond's program goes beyond predicting compatibility between the sun signs. Providing a thorough introduction to astrology, he helps beginners decipher their birth charts and understand what the planets reveal about their hopes, fears, needs, and skills relating to relationships. Step-by-step techniques help you compare your chart to another's, revealing the harmonious and challenging aspects of your union. Includes an easy-to-use CD-ROM to calculate and interpret your intimate relationships.

0-7387-0420-2, 240-pp., 7½ x 9⅛ book, includes CD-ROM (version 1.1) for PC with Windows 95/98/ME/XP   **$19.95**

Astrology & Relationships
Techniques for Harmonious Personal Connections

DAVID POND

Take your relationships to a deeper level. There is a hunger for intimacy in the modern world. *Astrology & Relationships* is a guidebook on how to use astrology to improve all your relationships. This is not fortunetelling astrology, predicting which signs you will be most compatible with; instead, it uses astrology as a model to help you experience greater fulfillment and joy in relating to others. You can also look up your planets, and those of others, to discover specific relationship needs and talents.

What makes this book unique is that it goes beyond descriptive astrology to suggest methods and techniques for actualizing the stages of a relationship that each planet represents. Many of the exercises are designed to awaken individual skills and heighten self-understanding, leading you to first identify a particular quality within yourself, and then to relate to it in others.

0-7387-0046-0, 368 pp., 7½ x 9⅛ $17.95

To order, call 1-877-NEW-WRLD
Prices subject to change without notice

All Around the Zodiac
Exploring Astrology's Twelve Signs

Bil Tierney

A fresh, in-depth perspective on the zodiac you thought you knew. This book provides a revealing new look at the astrological signs, from Aries to Pisces. Gain a deeper understanding of how each sign motivates you to grow and evolve in consciousness. How does Aries work with Pisces? What does Gemini share in common with Scorpio? *All Around the Zodiac* is the only book on the market to explore these sign combinations to such a degree.

Not your typical Sun sign guide, this book is broken into three parts. Part 1 defines the signs, part 2 analyzes the expression of sixty-six pairs of signs, and part 3 designates the expression of the planets and houses in the signs.

0-7387-0111-4, 528 pp., 6 x 9 $17.95

To order, call 1-877-NEW-WRLD
Prices subject to change without notice

You Are Psychic
The Art of Clairvoyant Reading & Healing

DEBRA LYNNE KATZ

Learn to see inside yourself and others. Clairvoyance is the ability to see information—in the form of visions and images—through nonphysical means. According to Debra Lynne Katz, anyone who can visualize a simple shape, such as a circle, has clairvoyant ability.

In *You Are Psychic*, Katz shares her own experiences and methods for developing these clairvoyant skills. Her techniques and psychic tools are easy to follow and have been proven to work by long-time practitioners. Psychic readings, healing methods, vision interpretation, and spiritual counseling are all covered in this practical guide to clairvoyance.

0-7387-0592-6, 336 pp., 6 x 9, illus. $14.95

To order, call 1-877-NEW-WRLD
Prices subject to change without notice

Practical Guide to Past-Life Memories
Twelve Proven Methods

RICHARD WEBSTER

Past life memories can provide valuable clues as to why we behave the way we do. They can shed light on our purpose in life, and they can help us heal our current wounds. Now you can recall your past lives on your own, without the aid of a hypnotist. This book includes only the most successful and beneficial methods used in the author's classes. Since one method does not work for everyone, you can experiment with twelve different straightforward techniques to find the best one for you.

This book also answers many questions, such as "Do I have a soul mate?", "Does everyone have a past life?", "Is it dangerous?", and "What about déjà vu?"

0-7387-0077-0, 264 pp., 5¾₆ x 8   **$9.95**

To order, call 1-877-NEW-WRLD
Prices subject to change without notice

click. click. click.

- ◉ *online bookstore*
- ◉ *free web tarot*
- ◉ *astrology readings*
- ◉ *moon phases*
- ◉ *spell-a-day*
- ◉ *new age encyclopedia*
- ◉ *articles*
- ◉ *the kitchen sink*

www.llewellyn.com

l l e w e l l y n w o r l d w i d e